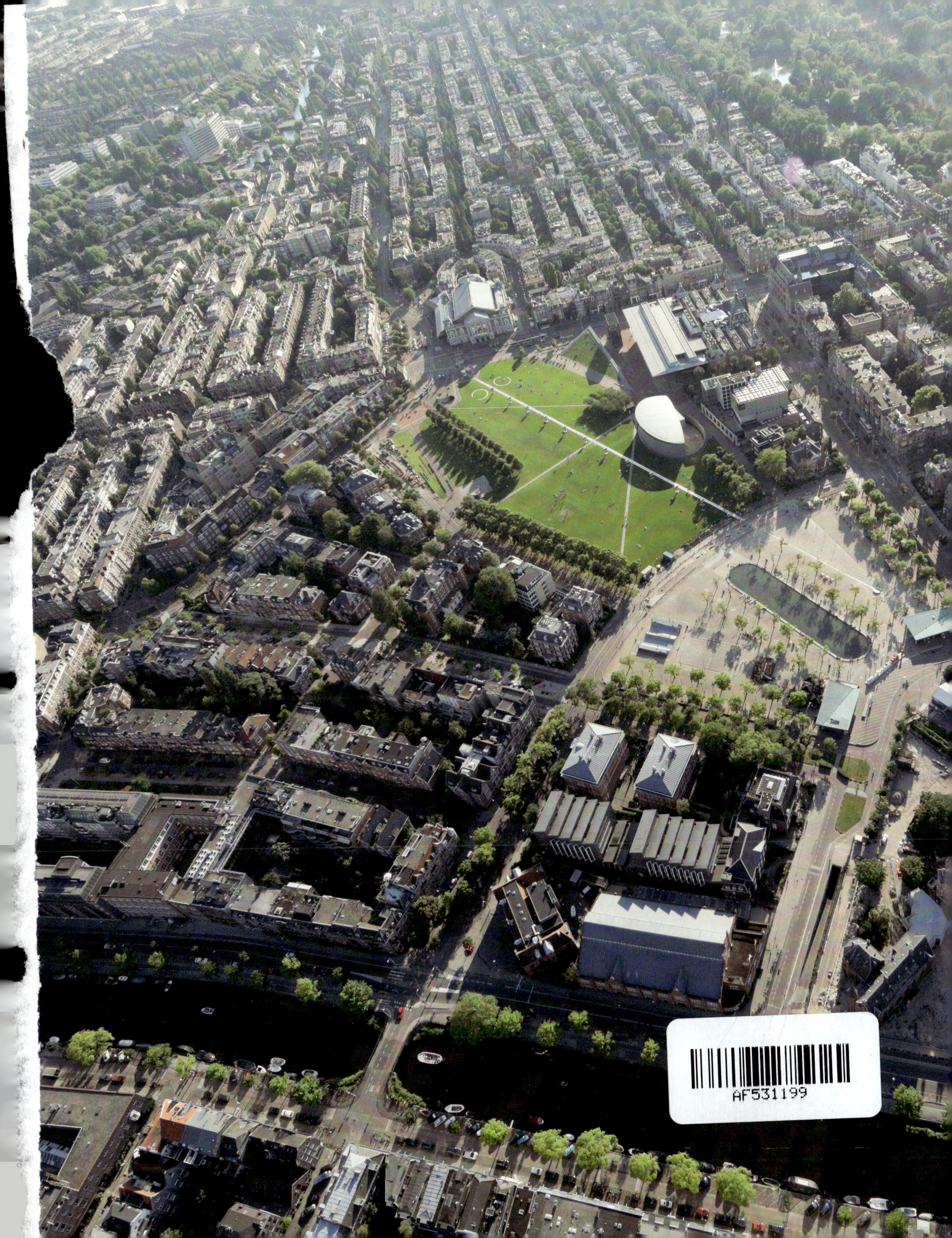

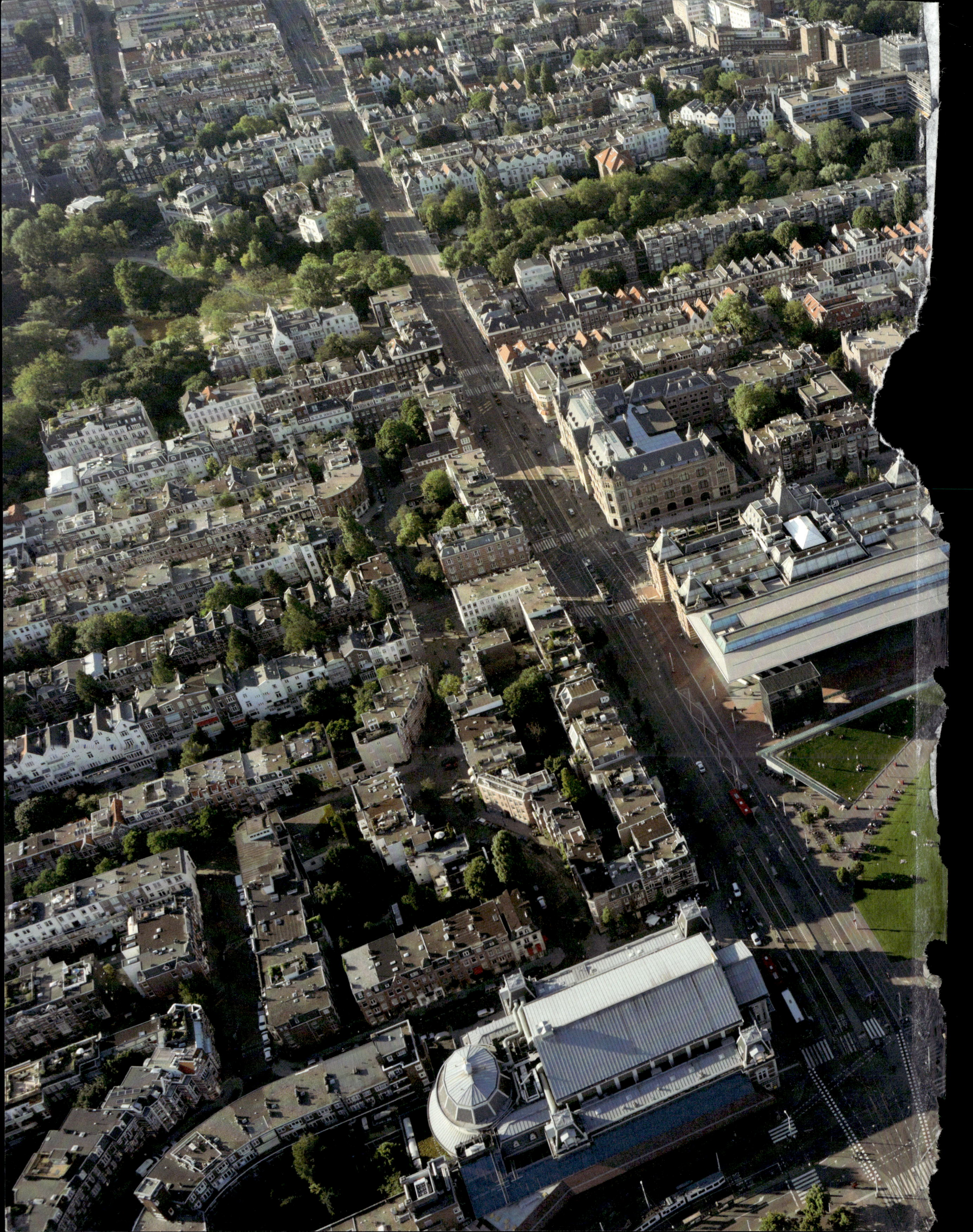

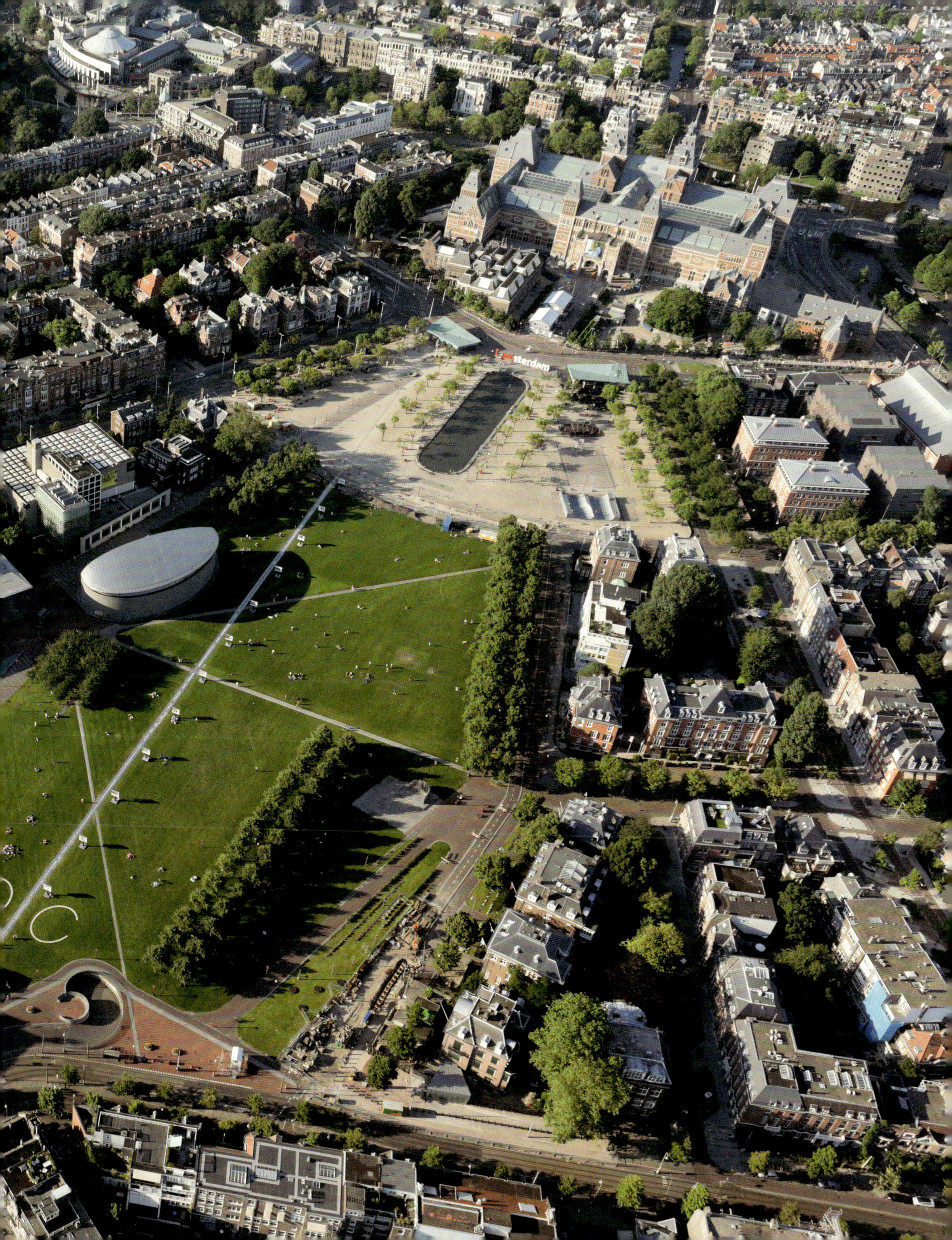

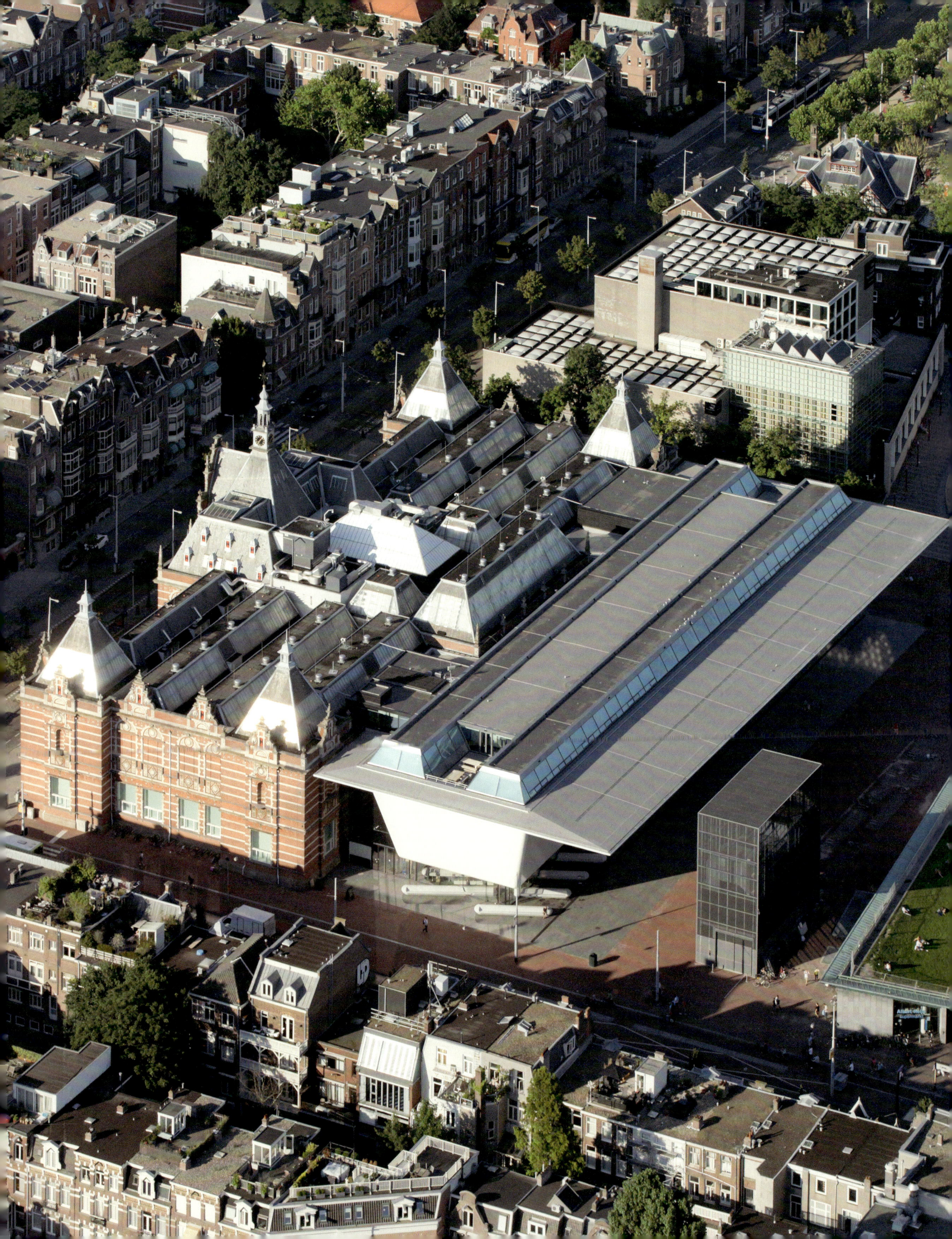

Stedelijk Architecture

Content

Stedelijk Museum Amsterdam / nai010 Publishers

Foreword

This publication celebrates the renovation and expansion of the Stedelijk Museum Amsterdam, the Netherlands' premiere institution for contemporary art and design, situated in the cultural heart of the city—the Museumplein. The original 19th-century building with its majestic staircase, grand galleries, and profuse natural lighting, designed by Adriaan Willem Weissman, has been carefully restored to its former glory. A spectacular new wing has been added to bring it firmly into the 21st Century with more space than ever to house our internationally renowned collection.

The Stedelijk Museum has been a home to art and artists since 1895, and the architecture as well as the institution it represents have been a continuous source of inspiration. Karel Appel painted murals onto the walls; Jan Dibbets excavated the building's four corners; Keith Haring created a velum ceiling painting, and Dan Flavin produced a site-specific monumental fluorescent light installation to fill the grand entry staircase. This building has also shaped our memories and experiences of art, whether in encounters with geometric abstractions by Kazimir Malevich in the intimate display cabinets or with Willem de Kooning's sweeping gestures, which match the grandeur of the Hall of Honor. While the building was closed for renovation and expansion the Stedelijk's curators have gained a new appreciation for how inextricably linked the building is to its collection. For the last decade, we have ventured outside its walls, worked in temporary spaces in Amsterdam, loaned works to other museums throughout the world, forged new alliances, and worked with inspiring partners. Returning to the renovated museum, however, began a very special episode in the museum's history. In 2010, the Temporary Stedelijk at the Stedelijk Museum and the exhibitions *Taking Place* and *Making Histories* provided long-awaited opportunities to rediscover the museum's galleries and to reconnect with the art, the artists, the collection, and our visitors.

The grand reopening in 2012 brought us home to one of the most important collections of modern and contemporary art and design in the world. Because of the addition of the new wing, the Stedelijk boasts one of Amsterdam's largest exhibition spaces—1,100 square meters—a bustling museum shop, a state-of-the-art information center and library, and a restaurant with a wonderful terrace on the Museumplein.

Benthem Crouwel Architects designed the new wing, creating a sleek white, 3,000-square-meter façade made of composite material, in what is regarded as a modern feat of architectural engineering. The tenet that shapes all of Benthem Crouwel's architecture—that a building should always reflect the era in which it is built—is apparent in the new Stedelijk, especially in the experimental use of materials.

Stedelijk Architecture gives insight into the fascinating history of this museum through an essay by architecture critic Hans Ibelings that outlines the original plans by A. W. Weissman and explores the relationship between the historic building and the new wing. The Stedelijk's original building was the product of the thriving late 19th-century Dutch economy, which transformed Amsterdam into a modern city where art and culture flourished. Three of the great cultural buildings that surround the Museumplein—the Rijksmuseum (1885), the Concertgebouw (1888), and the Stedelijk Museum (1895)—were erected during this time. Starting in the 1930s, the Stedelijk underwent a radical modernization under director Willem Sandberg, whose ideals of a light, open, and accessible institution included the decision to paint the walls white. The Stedelijk and the Museum of Modern Art in New York were two of the first museums in the world to hang art on all-white walls, and since then most other museums followed suit. In 1954, the museum opened its first new wing, the Sandberg Wing, made largely out of glass, connecting the galleries and the urban realm.

Although Sandberg's addition to the original building was jettisoned in favor of the new wing in 2012, Benthem Crouwel Architects applied a similar philosophy. The conviction that in today's city a fluent transition between public space and museum space was essential, they connected the museum more directly to the Museumplein by moving the entrance of the building from the side facing Paulus Potterstraat to the Museumplein side. It was this aspect of the proposal, with its distinctive yet careful balance between old and new, that swayed the jury to select Benthem Crouwel's design for this prestigious commission. The architects' expansion of the Stedelijk Museum is both respectful toward the historic building and entirely contemporary; it succeeded in manifesting the concept of "unity in duality" in an ingenious way.

Amsterdam-based photographer Iwan Baan provides the photography for *Stedelijk Architecture*; he has been recognized internationally for his outstanding architectural photography. His distinctive style—proclaimed a "remaking of the genre"—is characterized by the dynamism and energy that result from including people, context, and environment in his images. His photos of the Stedelijk Museum explore the striking architectural features of the exterior, as well as the subtle transition between old and new in the museum's interior spaces.

We are very proud to present this publication in our opening year and we are grateful to all those who have contributed to it. We wish to extend our foremost appreciation to Mels Crouwel, whose vision has literally turned the building and expanded it in a most natural way. My sincere gratitude also goes to Hans Gerson, whose enthusiasm and energy united the Dienst Maatschappelijke Ontwikkeling [Department of Social Development] of the City of Amsterdam, ABT, Audi, Benthem Crouwel Architekten BV, Royal HaskoningDHV, Imtech, VolkerWessels Bouw & Vastgoedontwikkeling West to make this book possible.

Additionally, we wish to thank Hans Ibelings and Iwan Baan for their inspiring and beautiful contributions, and Mevis & Van Deursen for their exceptional design.

We extend our sincerest gratitude to the City of Amsterdam for its enduring support of the Stedelijk Museum. I also wish to express our deepest appreciation to our sponsors, founders, and major donors for their generous contributions that made this publication possible. Finally, I extend our thanks to the Stedelijk Museum's Supervisory Board for their valued and encouraging support.

The Stedelijk Museum Amsterdam holds a special place in our lives and hearts. We come here for inspiration and discovery, amazement and curiosity, discussion and contemplation, and to meet a friend for a cup of coffee. With our reopening, we continue to serve as a lasting home for art, artists, and the public. We hope you will enjoy this publication and with it the new Stedelijk Museum, and that every visit will provide joy and inspiration far into the future.

Ann Goldstein
Artistic Director

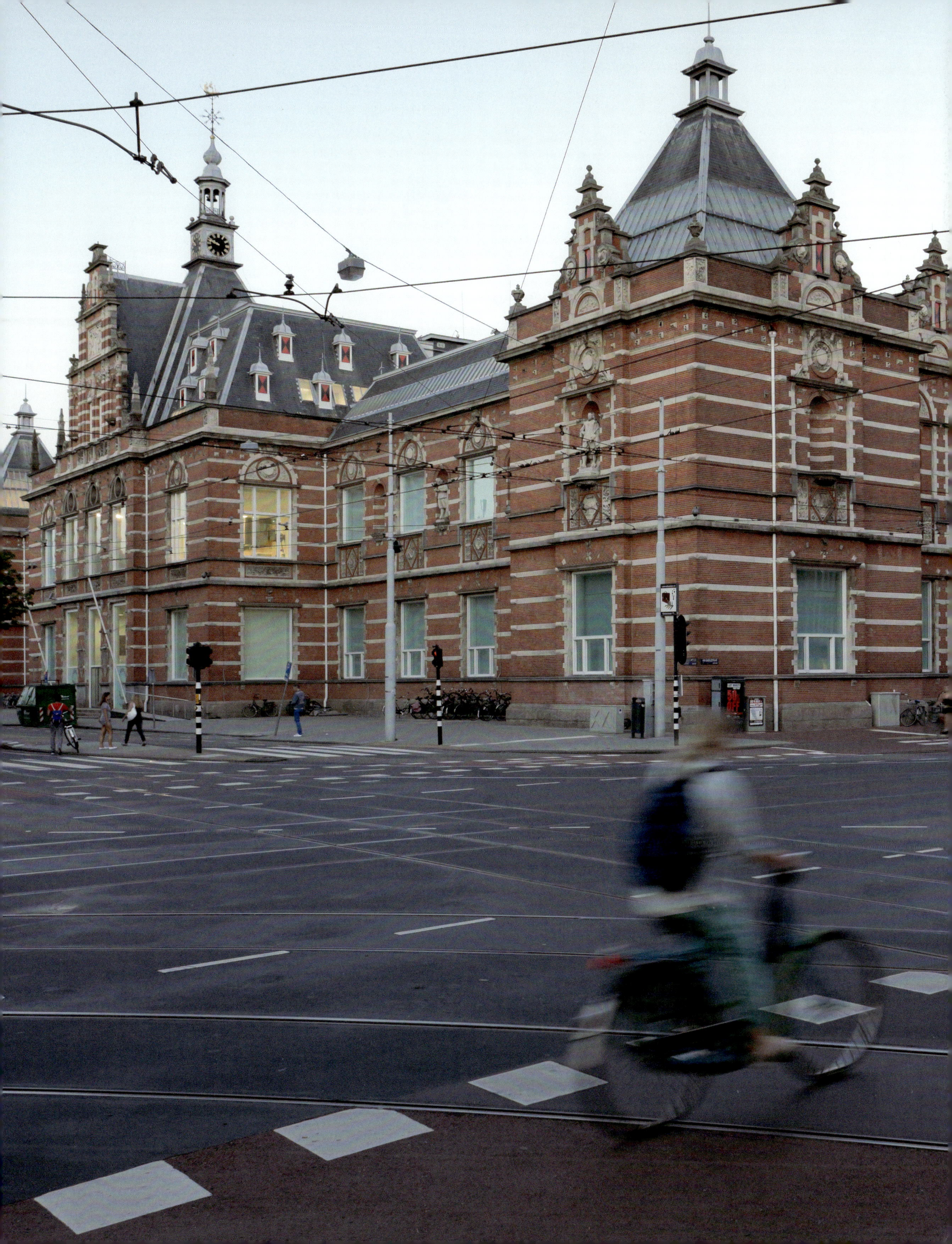

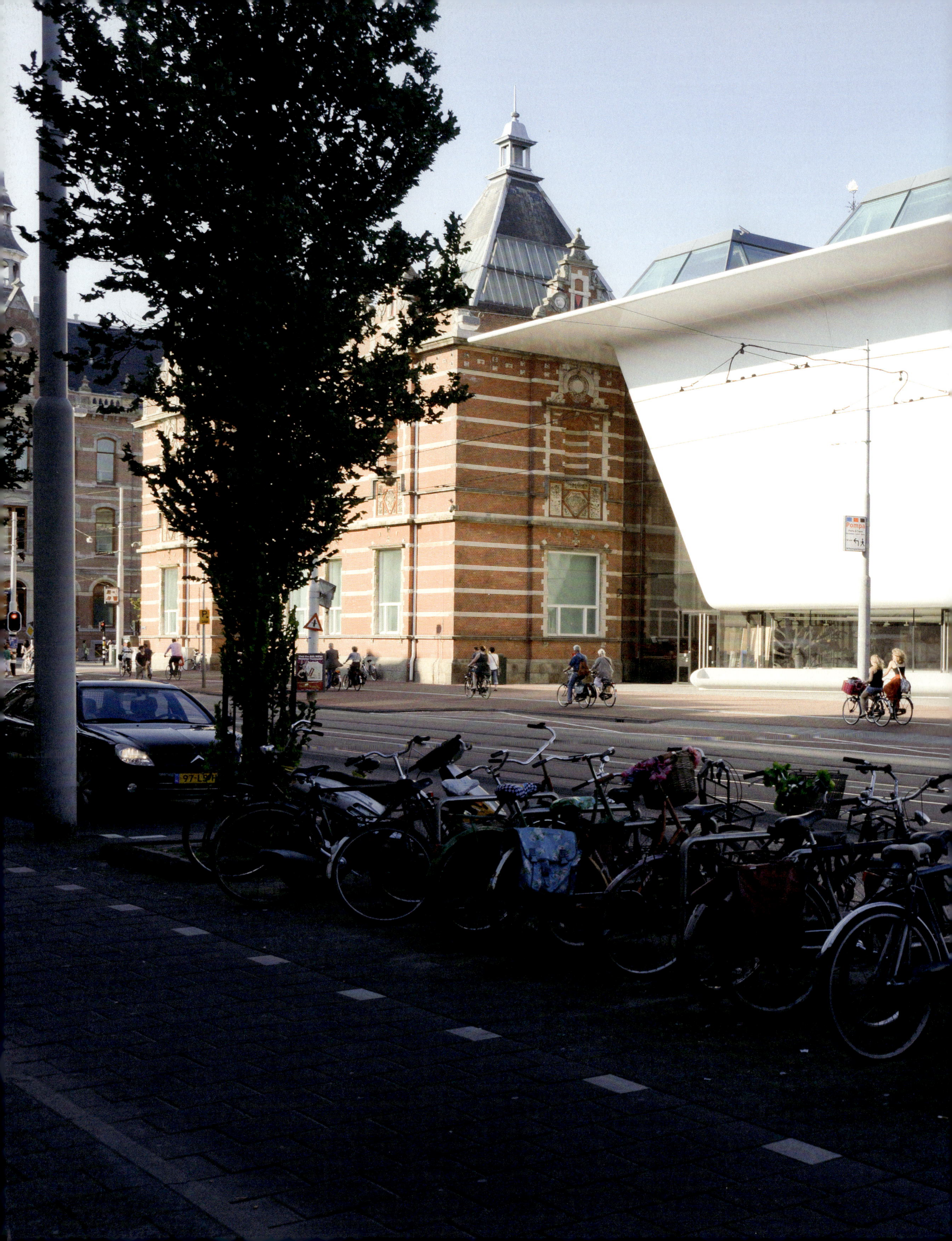
Pompa

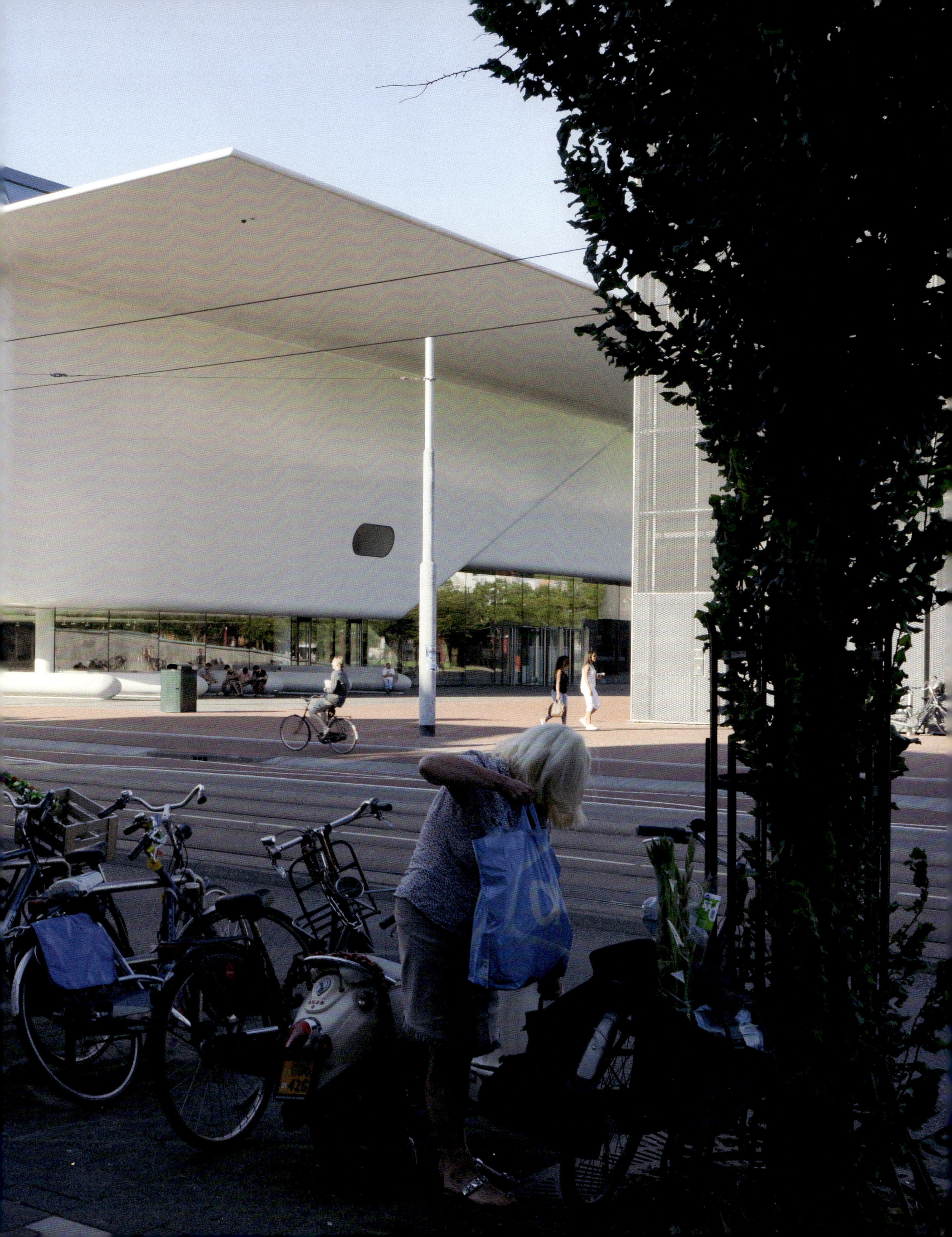

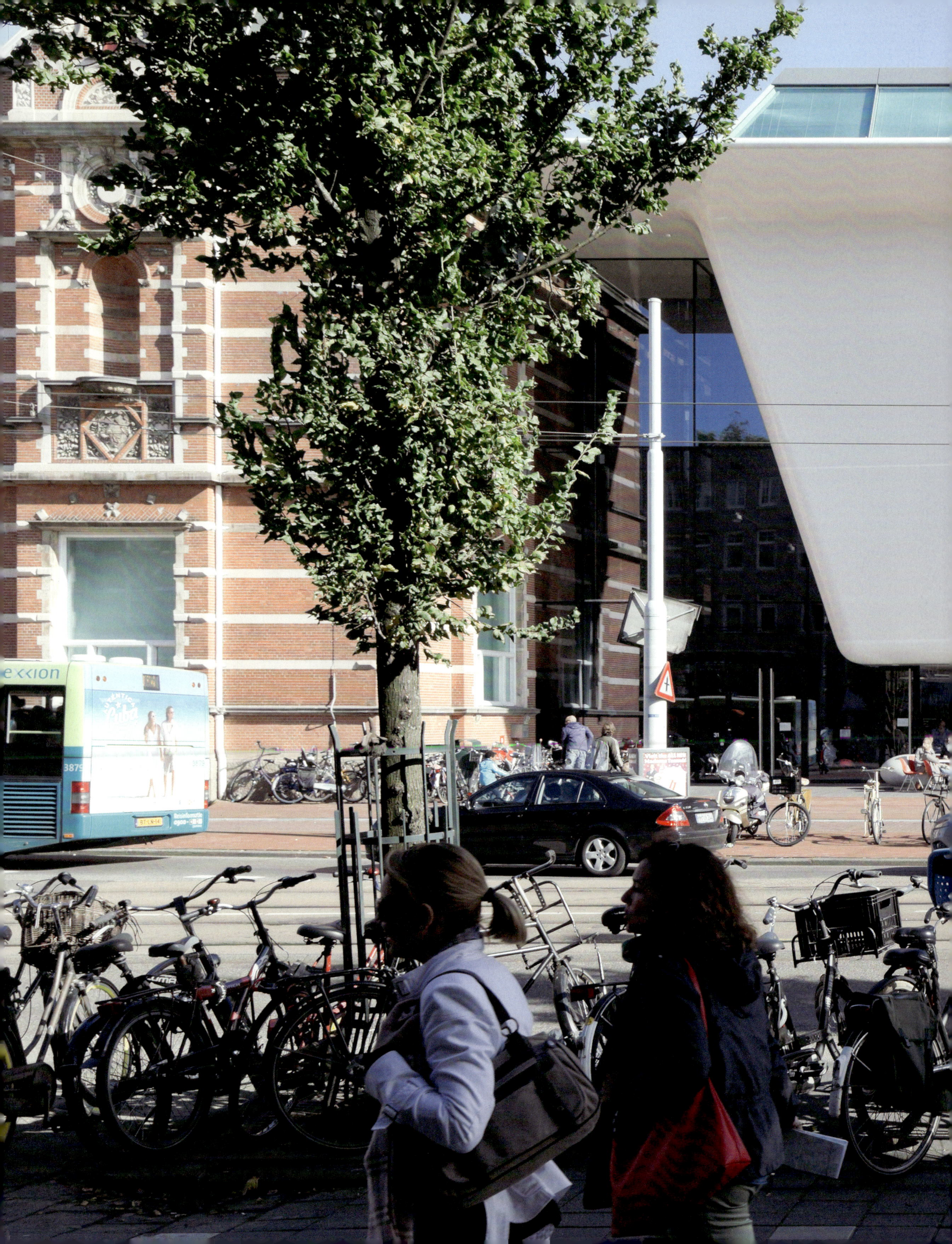

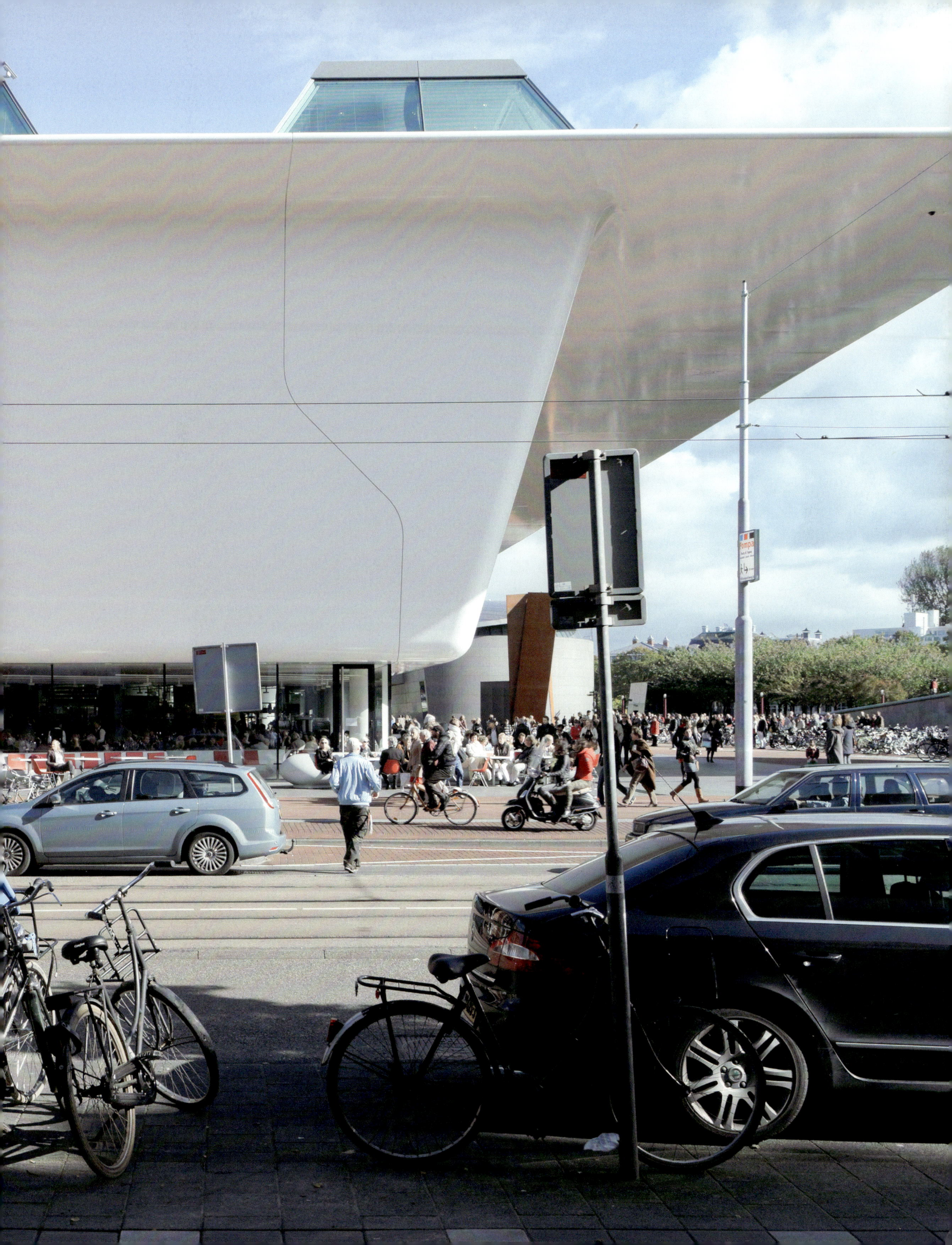

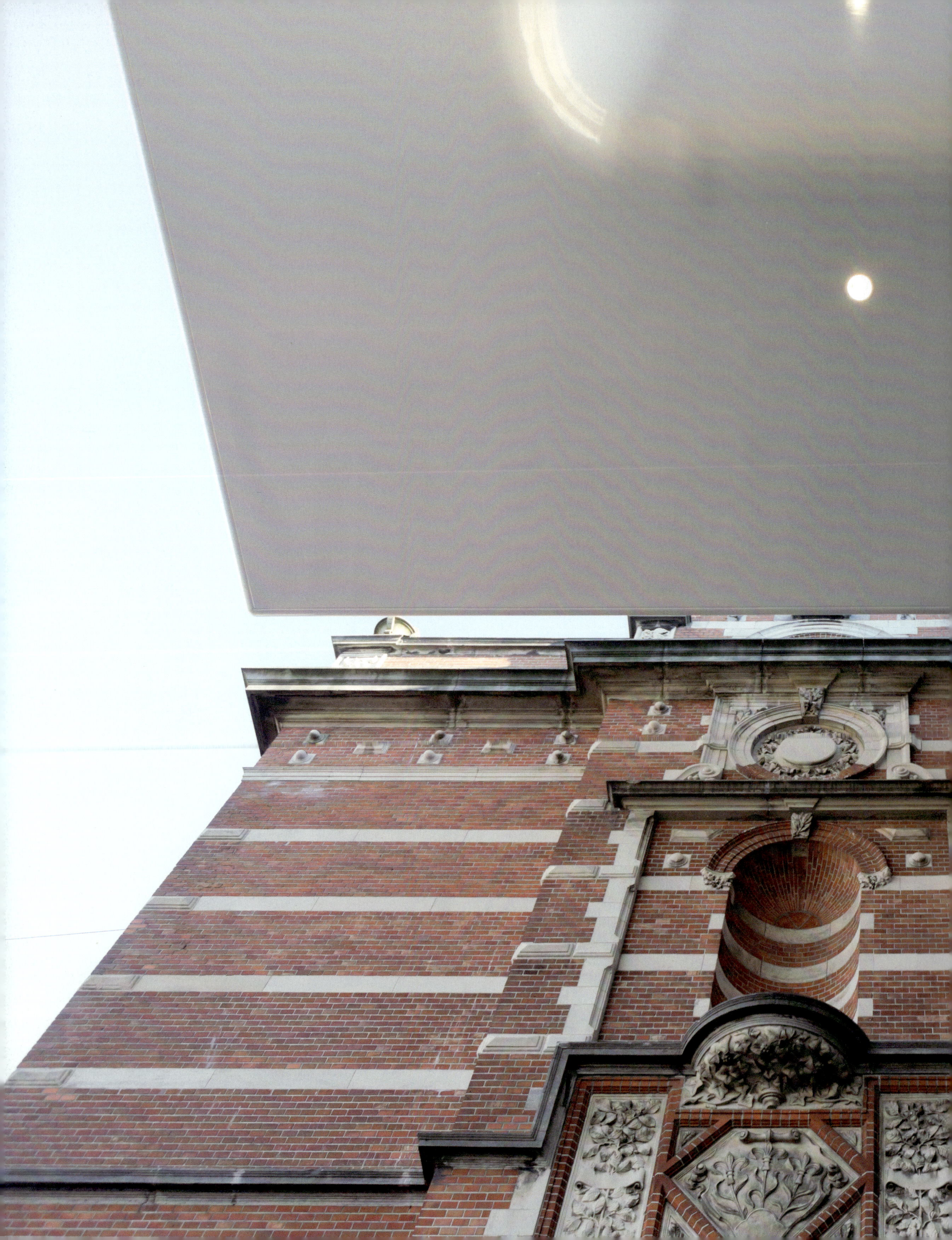

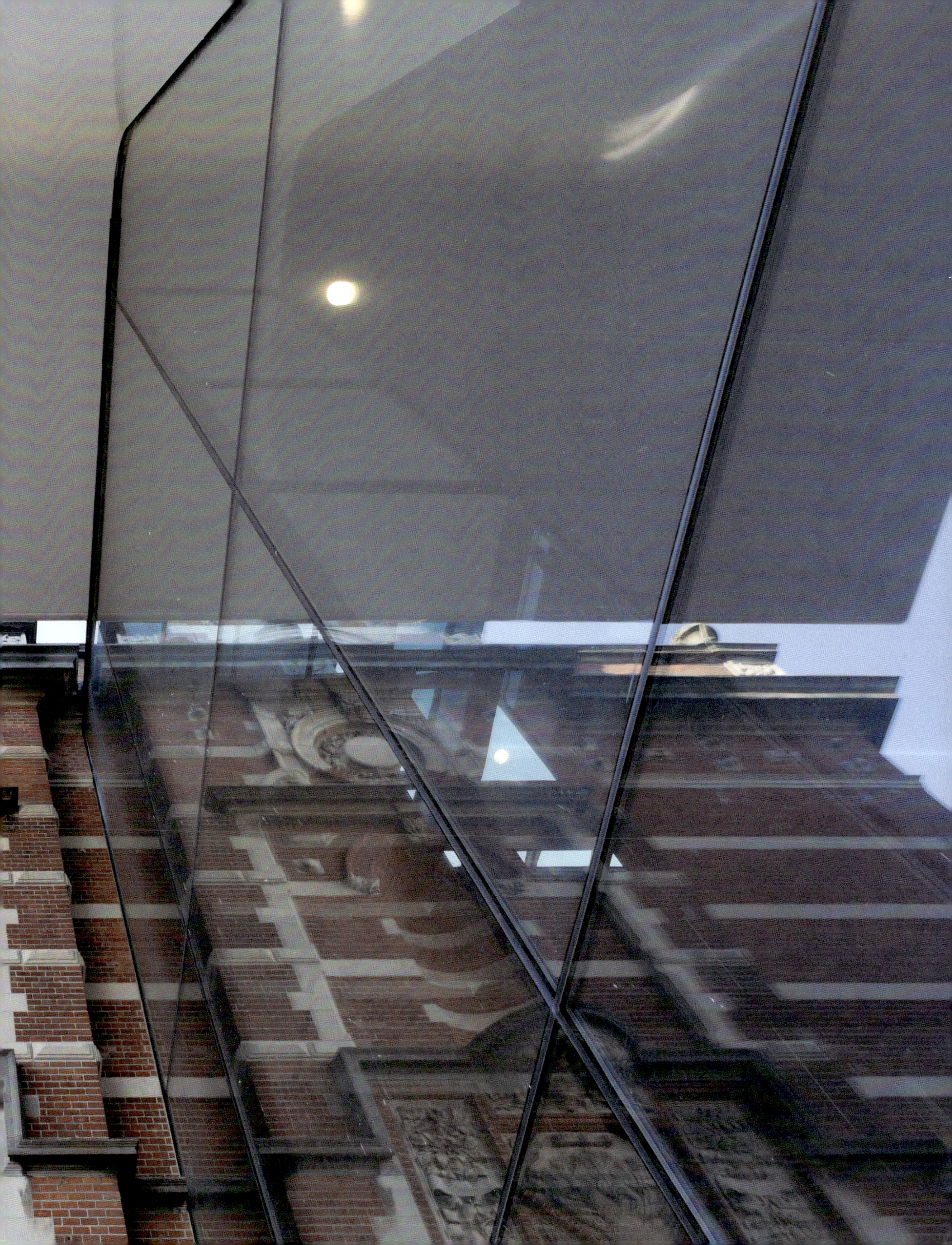

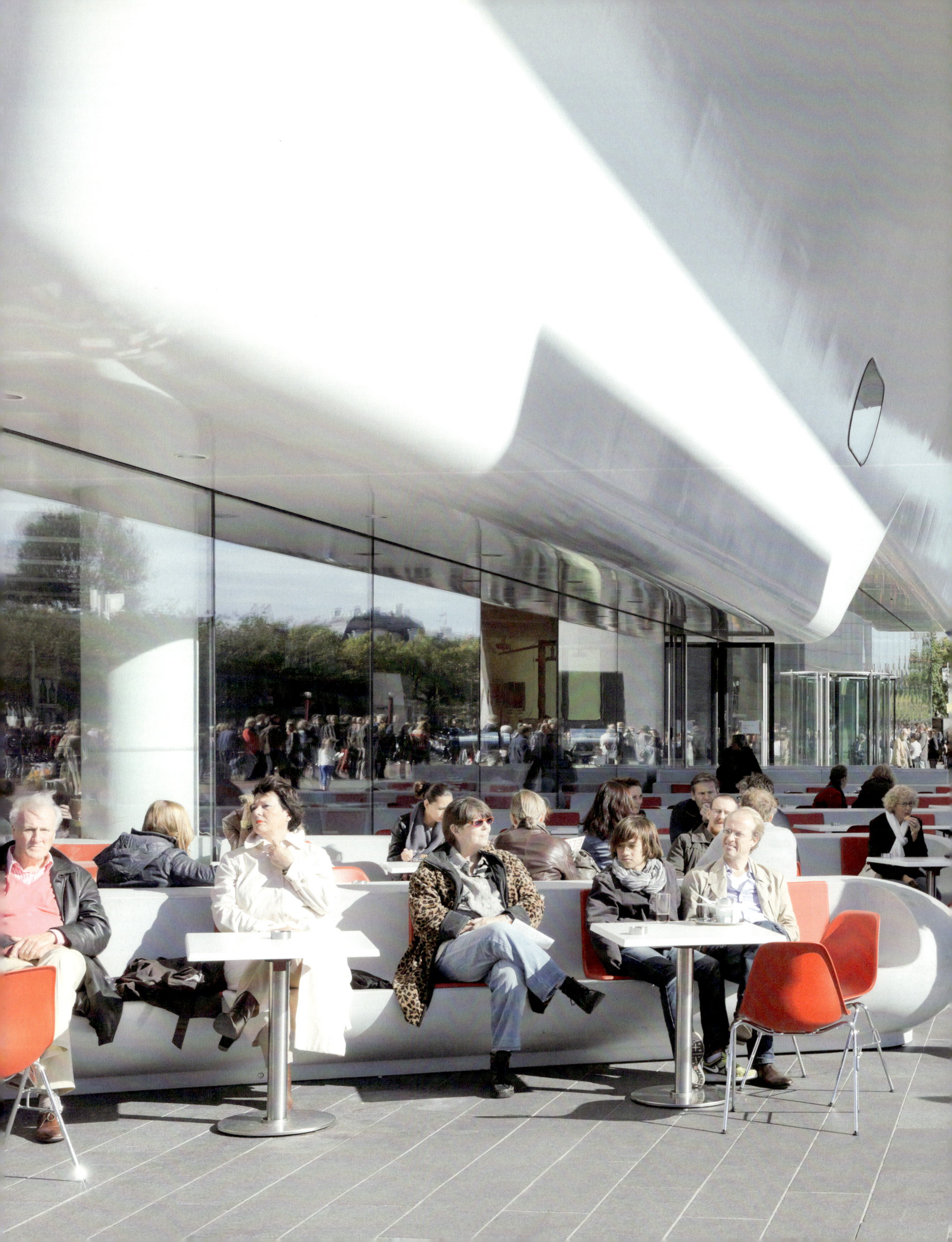

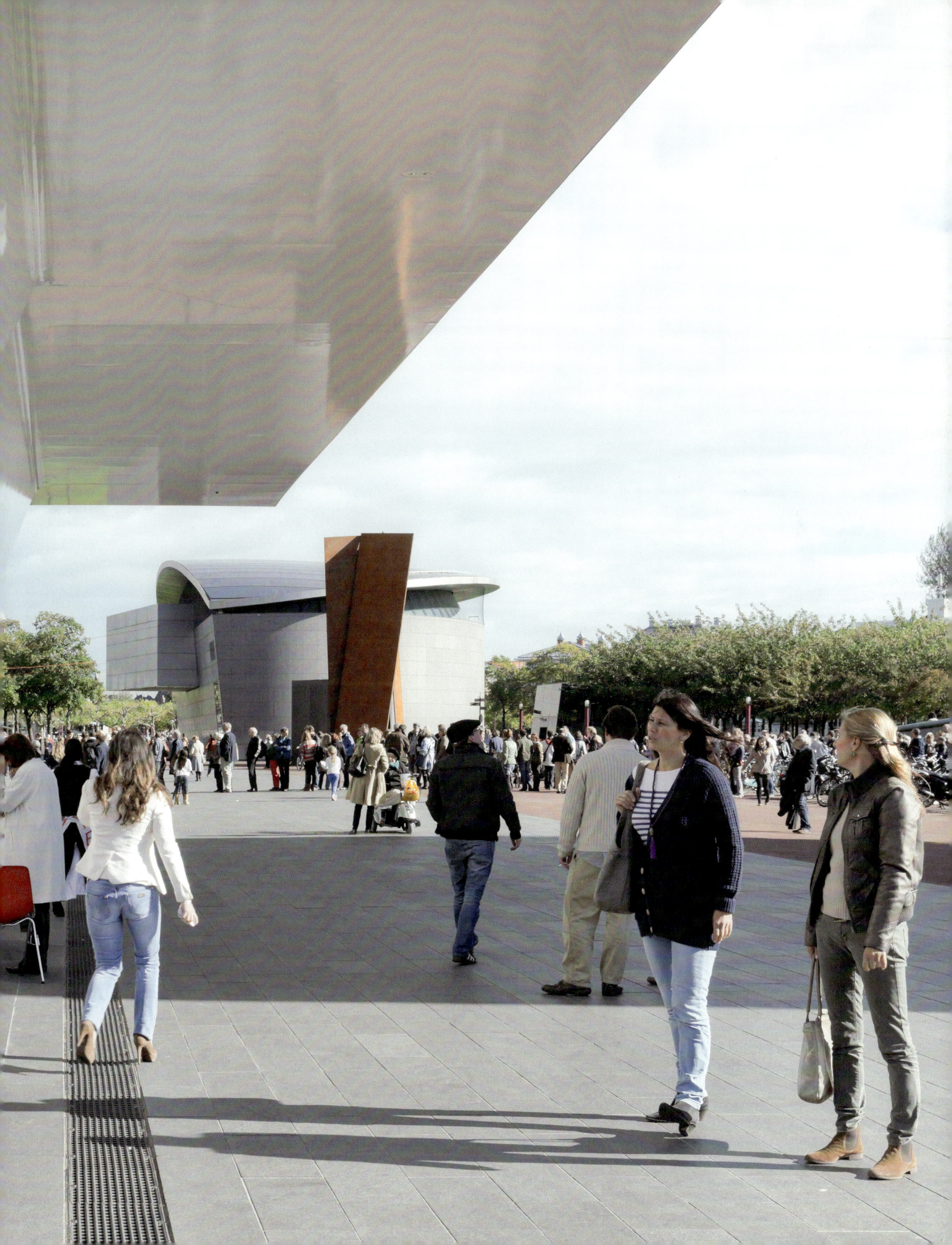

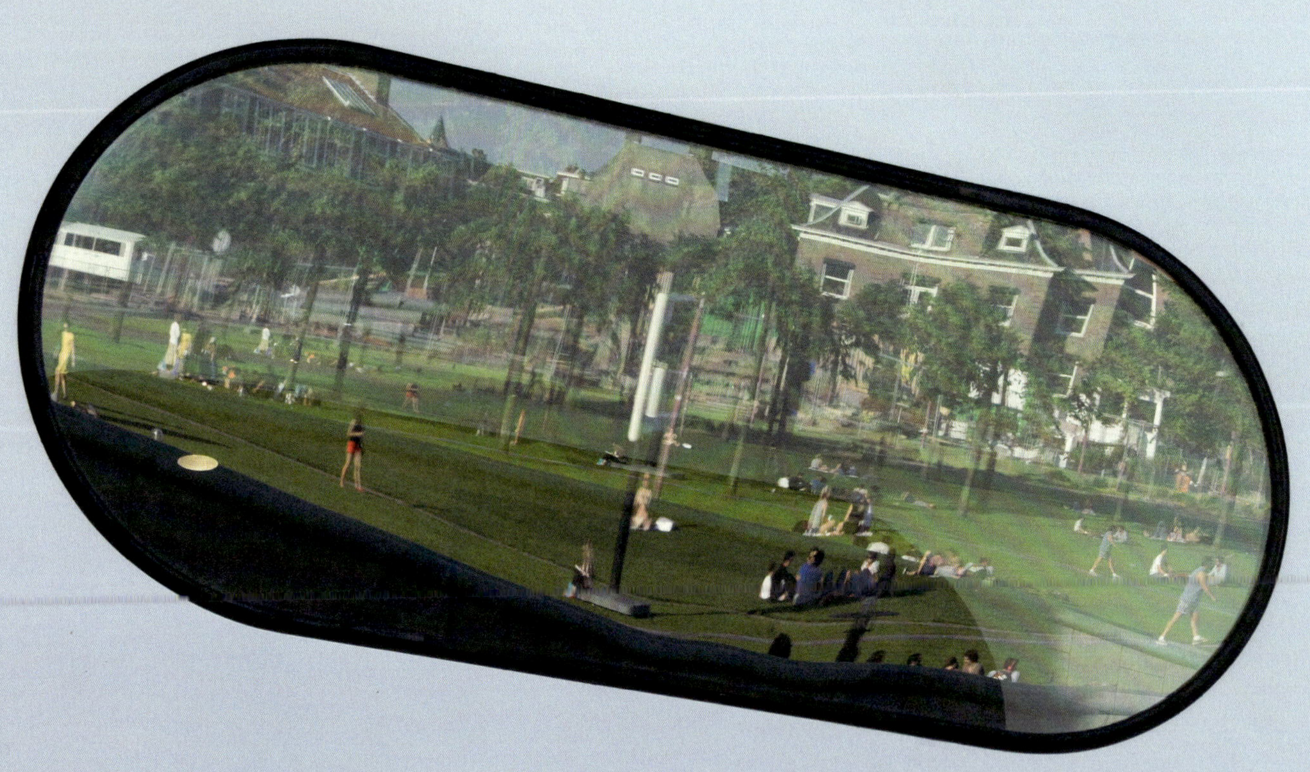

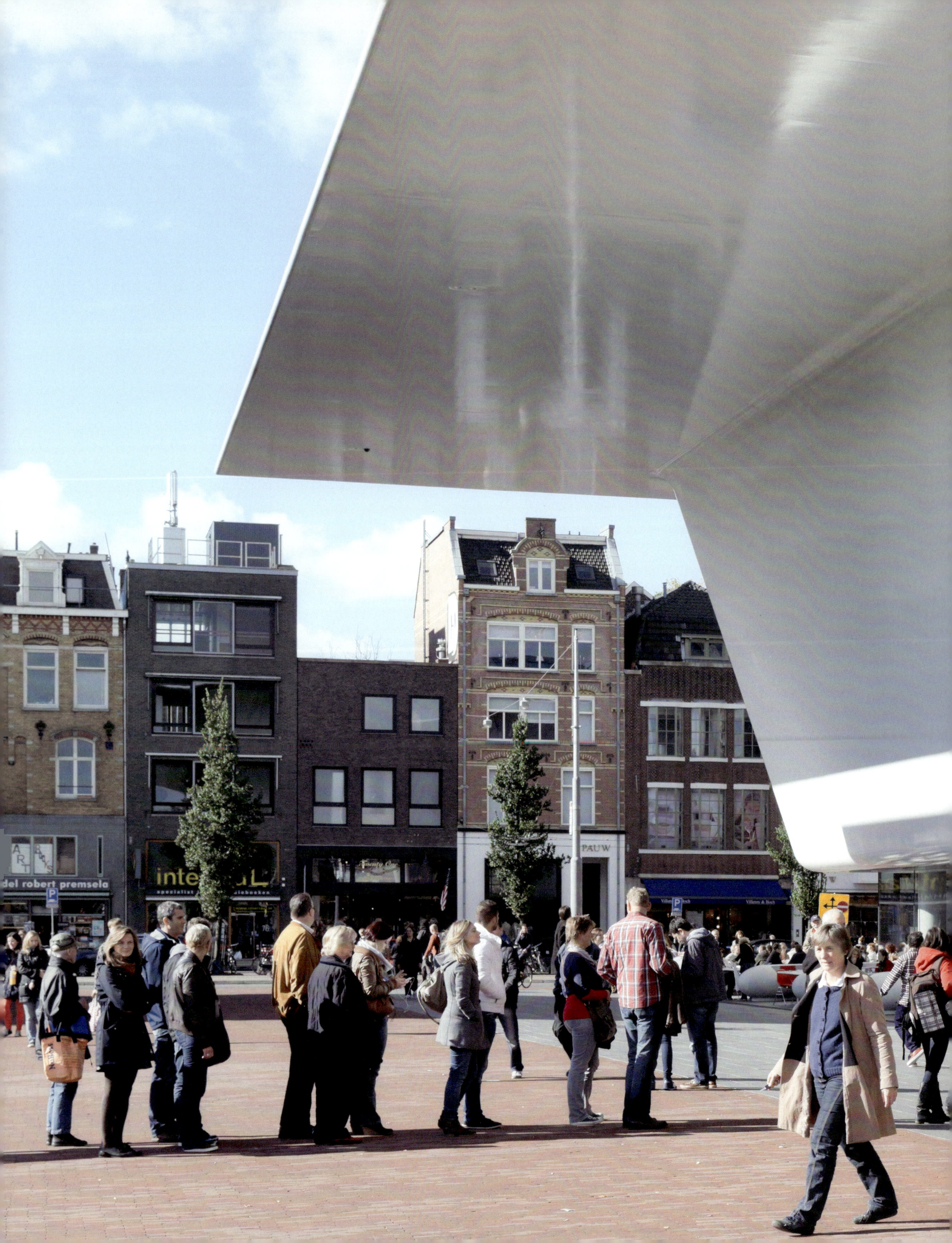
del robert premsela
P
PAUW

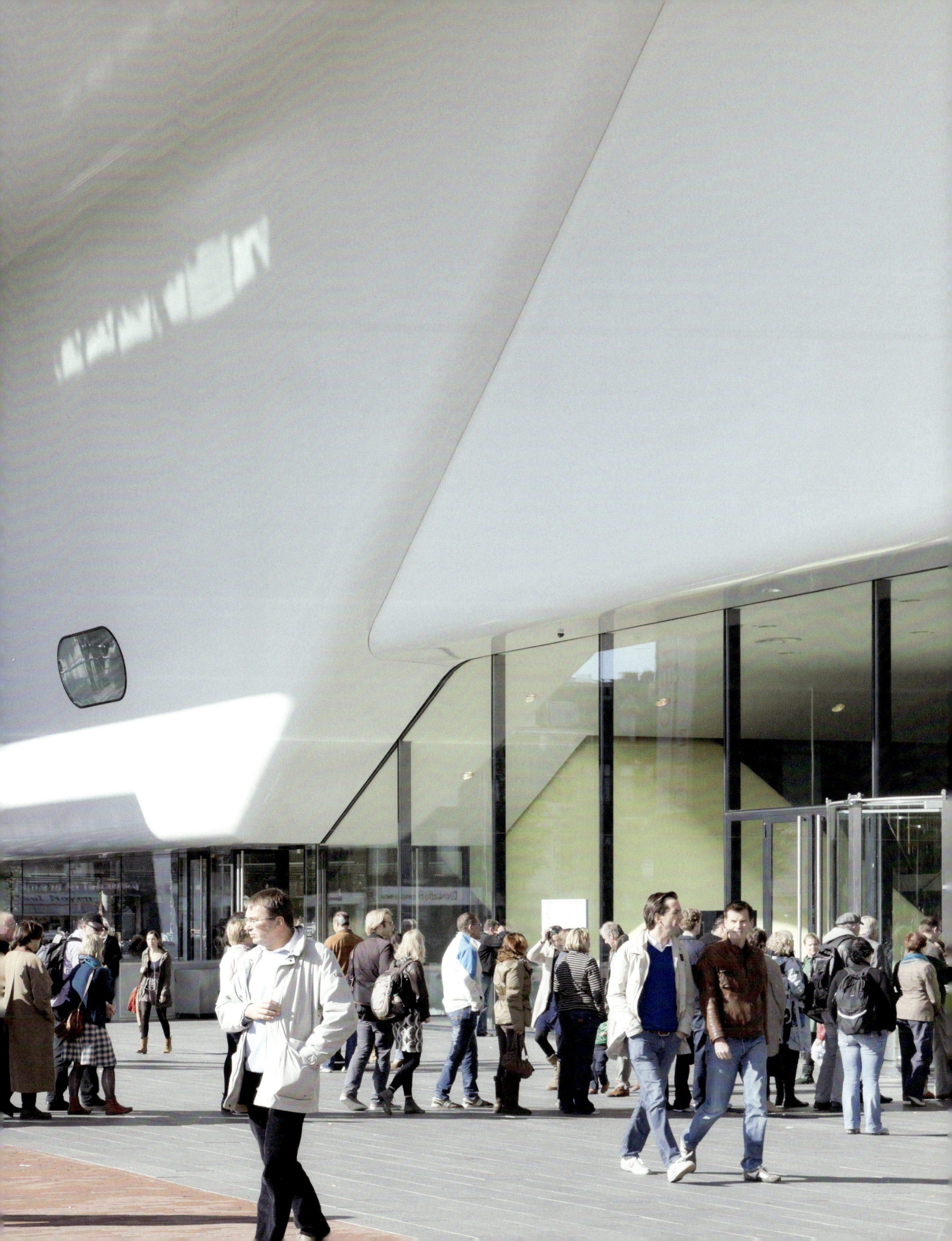

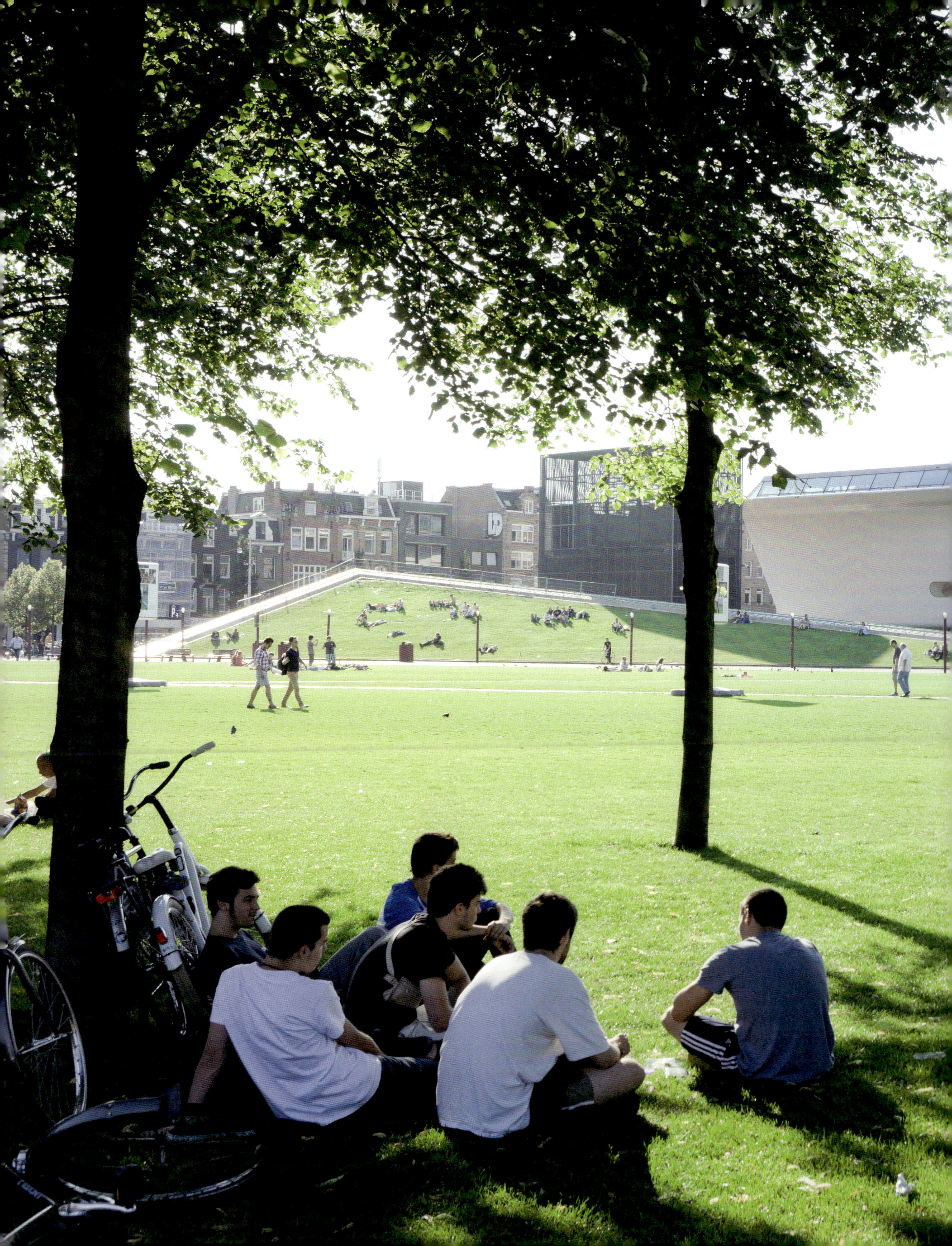

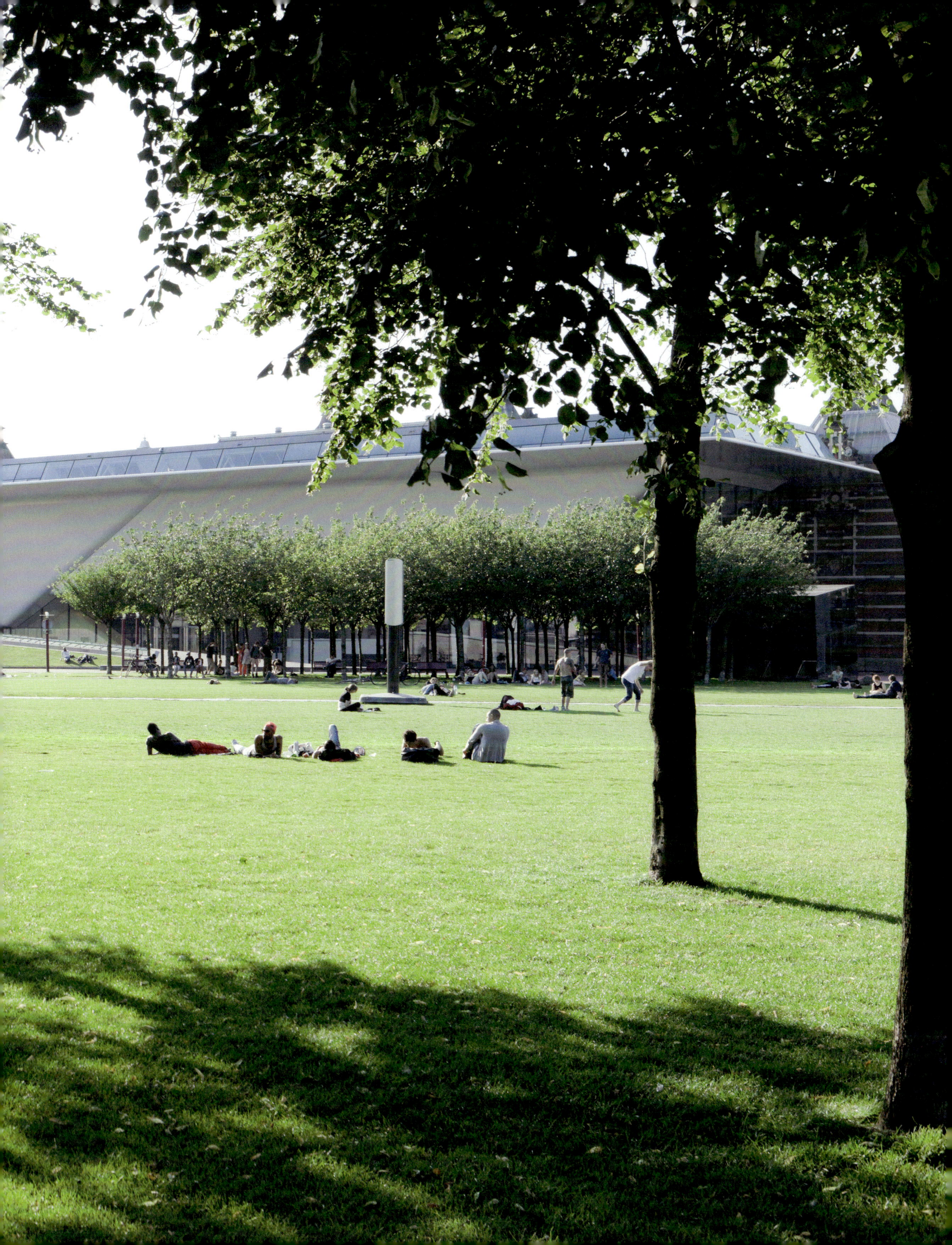

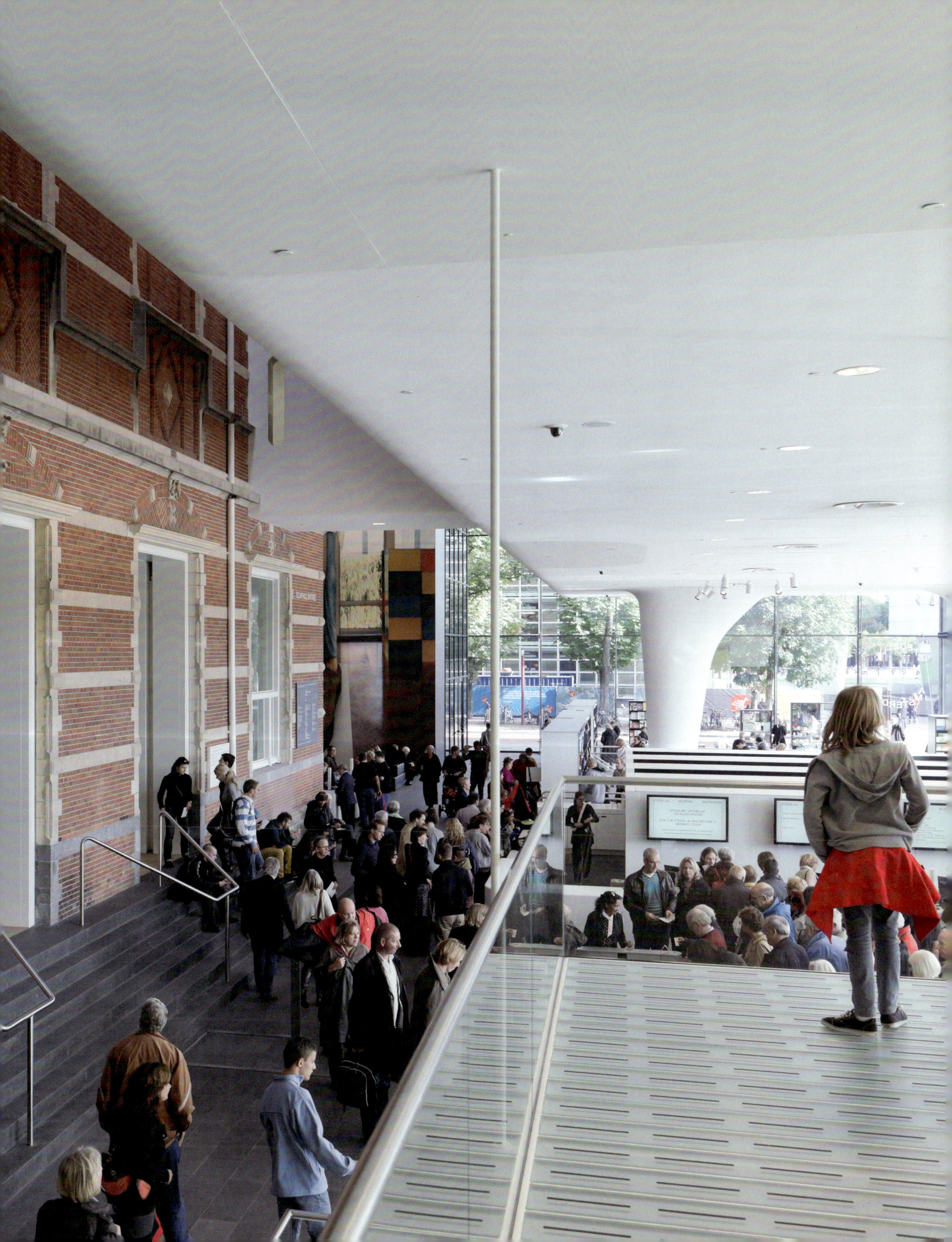

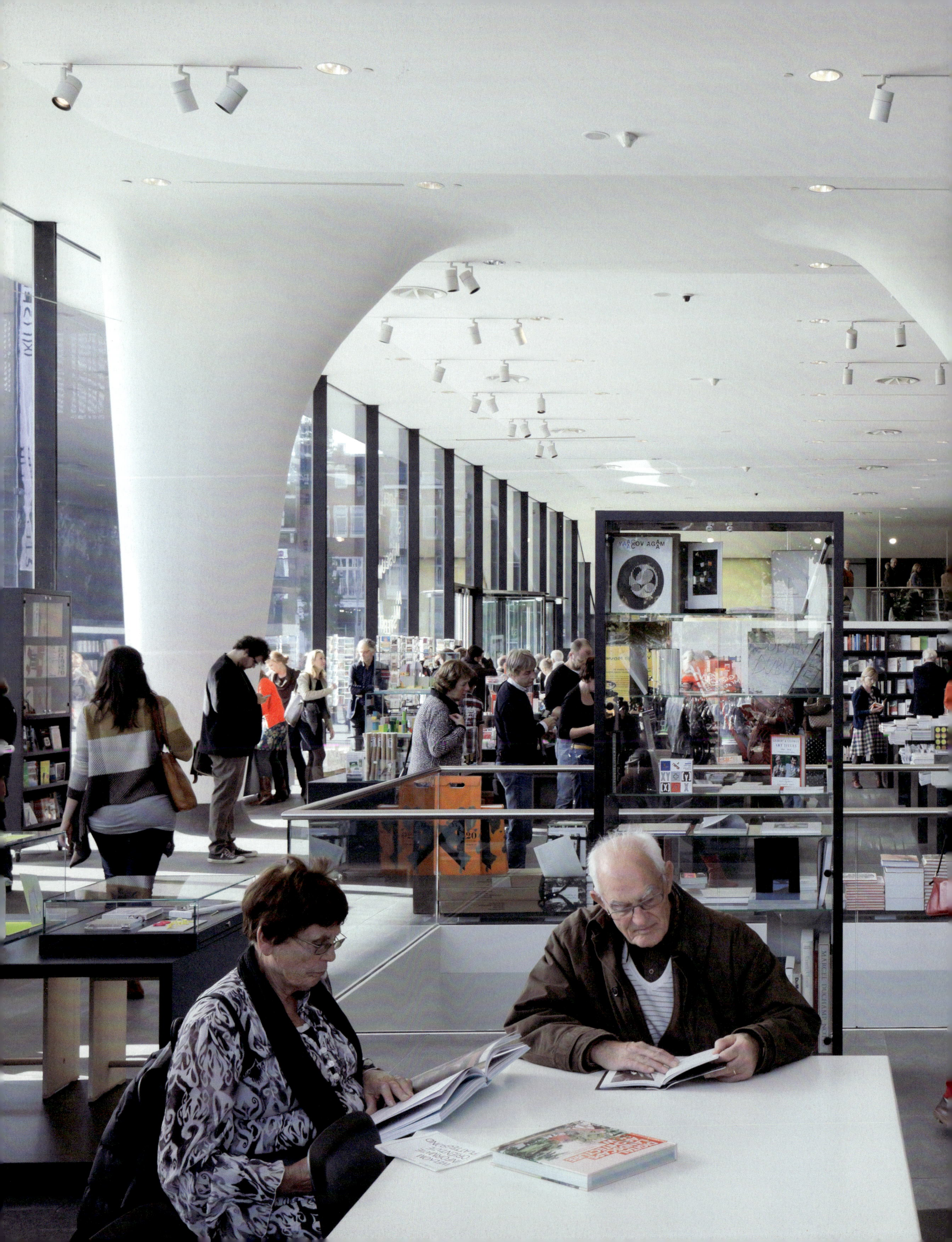

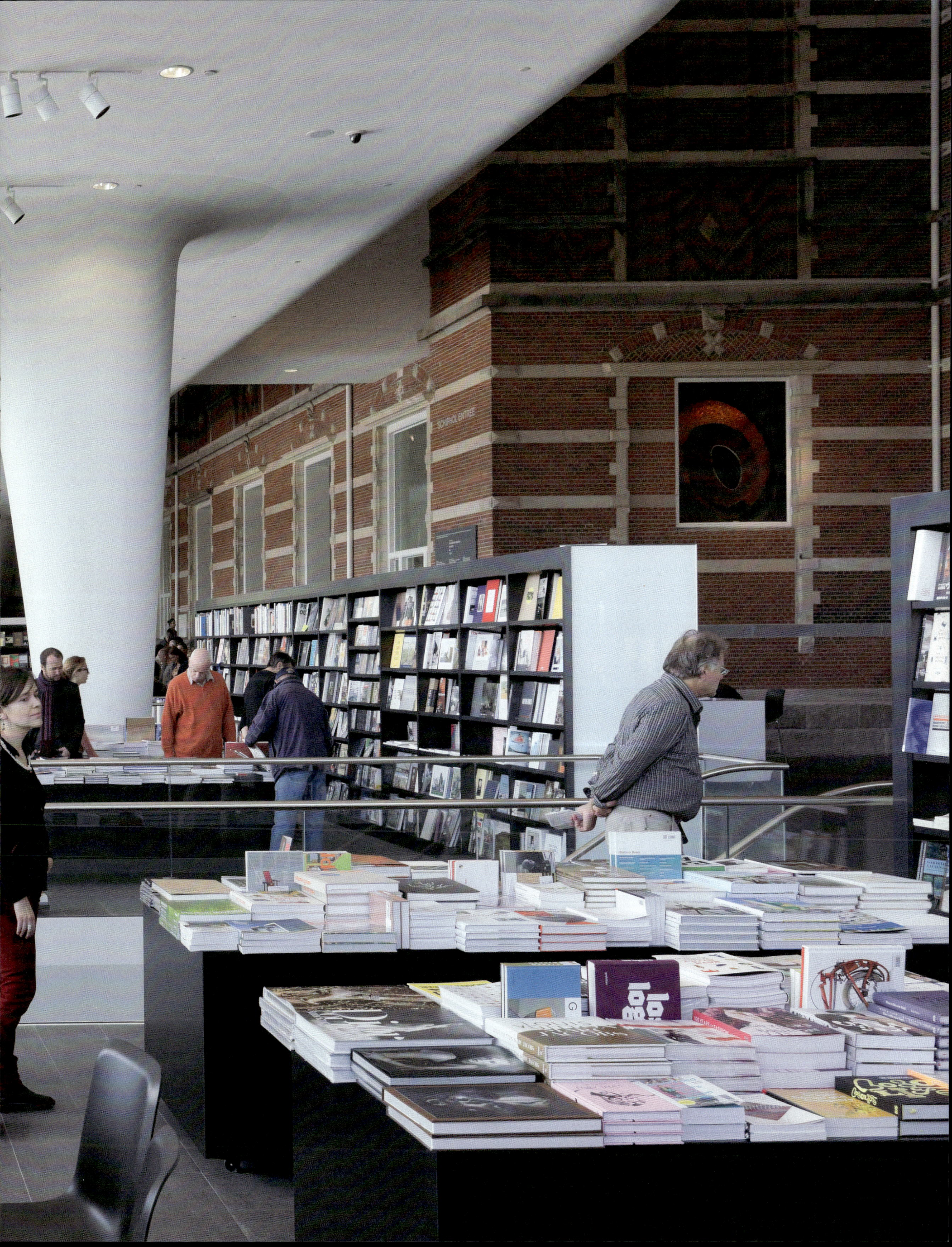

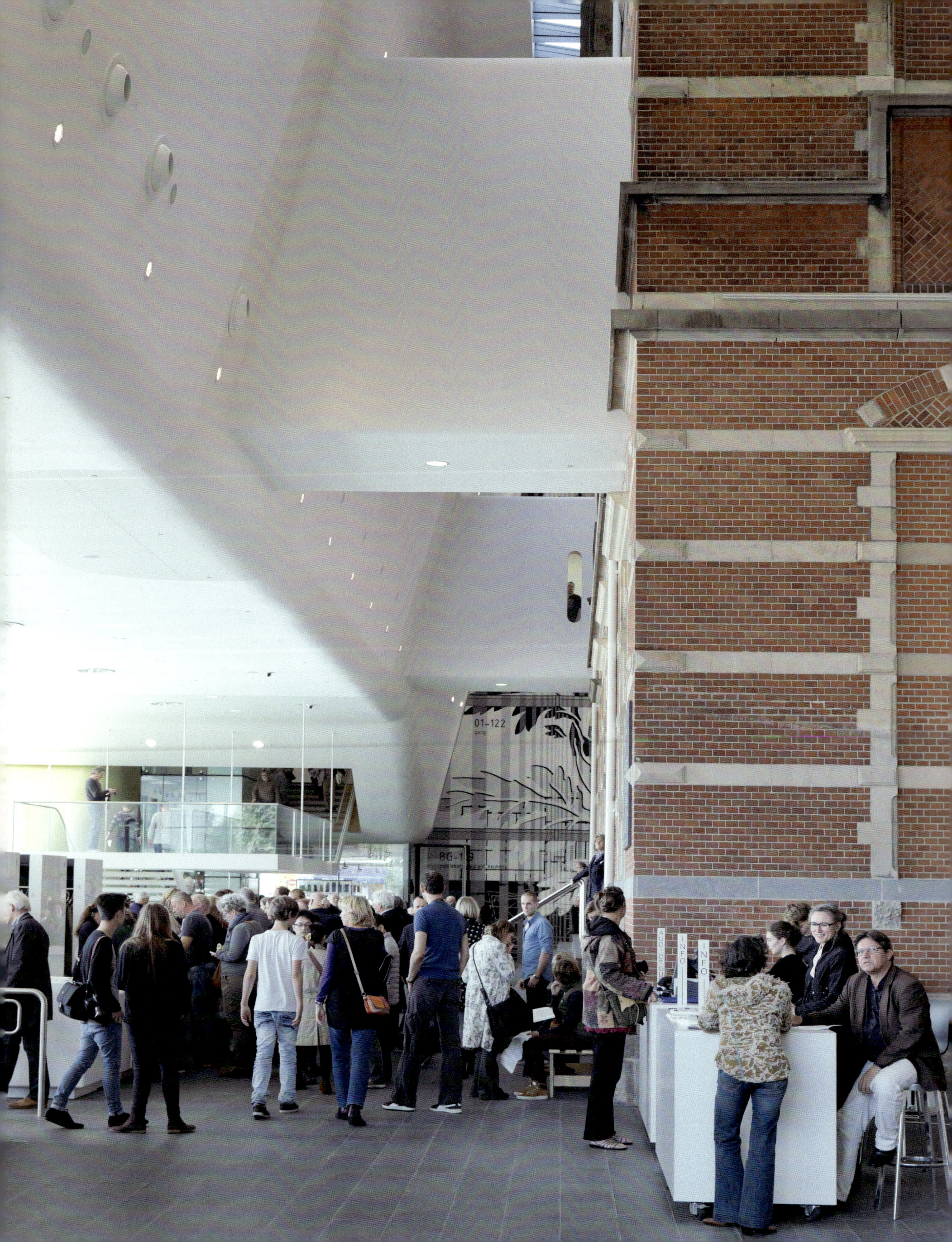
01–122
INFO
INFO

OLD AND NEW: A BALAN- CING ACT

Mels Crouwel on the architecture of the Stedelijk Museum

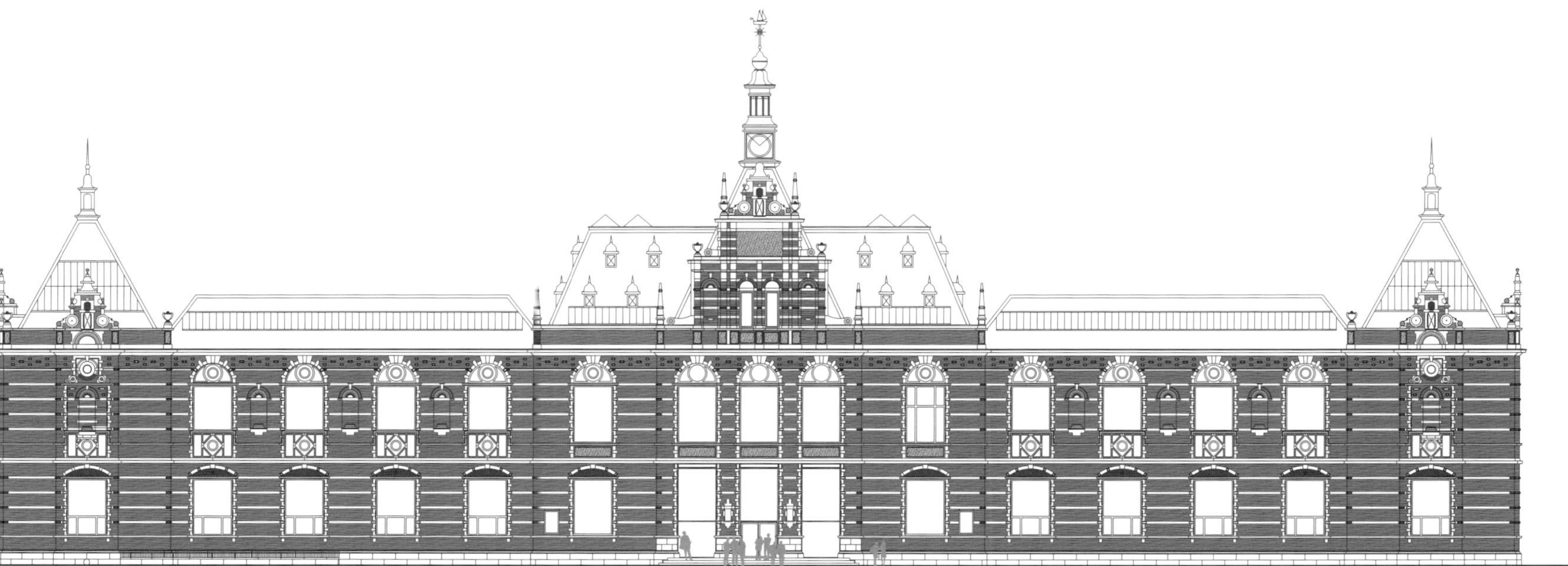

The North Façade: elevation

Mels Crouwel is one of the two of architects behind Benthem Crouwel Architects, the firm selected in the European tendering process to undertake the transformation of the Stedelijk Museum. Jan Benthem and Mels Crouwel began their collaboration in 1979. Their practice has been responsible for a large number and a great diversity of projects: Schiphol Airport, the transformation of the Rotterdam and Amsterdam railway stations, large office buildings, the Metro stations on Amsterdam's new North/South line and museums such as Foam and the Anne Frank House. Benthem Crouwel's work combines distinctive forms and contemporary materials and techniques with a cool expressiveness. The smooth, seamless white volume floating above the entrance to the Stedelijk Museum typifies Benthem Crouwel's approach.

Hans Ibelings: How did you deal with the existing building?

Mels Crouwel: "The Stedelijk Museum was purpose-built in 1895, symmetrical in layout, with paneling and ornamentation throughout, and with lovely overhead lighting on the first floor. In the 1930s, while the museum's director was away on holiday, Willem Sandberg had part of the interior painted white, and this treatment was later extended. This whitewashing of the interior is of some significance in the history of the building. Earlier modern art in particular was generally created at a time when exhibition spaces were not yet white. I value the fact that one can still discern some of the original details, and so experience the character of A. W. Weissman's architecture. We consciously decided to allow the history of the building to be seen where no art is on display. So the terrazzo floors were restored and we repaired the damaged arches in front of which display cases once stood. We stripped out the print gallery, which had been installed halfway up the stairs. We haven't sought to disguise the fact that the original building dates from 1895, and in the same spirit we have simply attempted to make the new structure a building of today. Looking at the exterior you see two buildings: one from 1895 and one from 2012. The entrance hall has been given the façade of the old building as a rear wall. In this way we have made optimal use of the time difference. Inside, however, our use of precisely the same treatment for the rooms means that you are hardly aware that you are moving from the old into the new, except perhaps if you look out of the small window, which we have made in the pedestrian walkways."

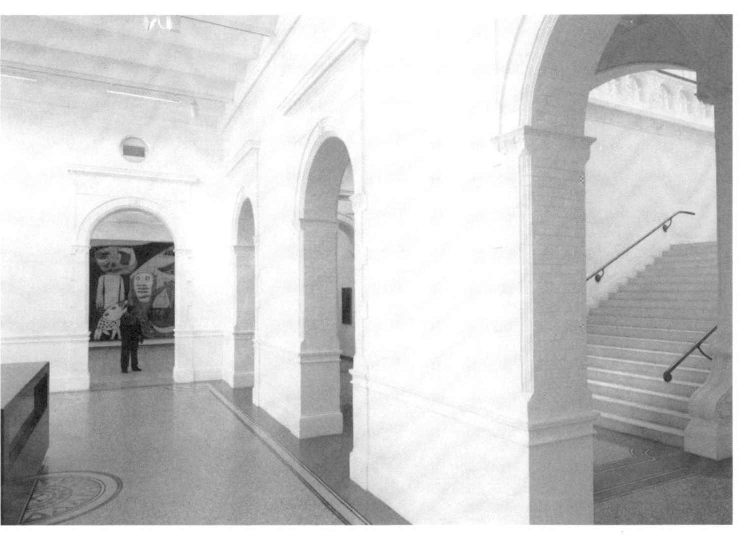

The restored terrazzo floor and arches in the former entrance lobby on the Paulus Potter street side of the building. "I value the fact that one can still discern some of the original details, and so experience the character of A. W. Weissman's architecture."

What did you add?

“As architects we felt that the building should not dominate the art. We wanted to make a building to optimize the display of the artworks, mediated of course by our own vision. In the past, paintings predominated, but contemporary art often involves installations, which are often best placed in virtually anonymous spaces. So our choice was to create fairly neutral spaces, while still retaining the old Stedelijk Museum.

The form of the rooms as well as the light must be extremely functional in a museum, and the Stedelijk Museum, known for the beautiful overhead light on the first floor, the lovely display cabinets and the simple succession of spaces, met these requirements more than adequately. It’s a building where you wouldn’t easily get lost, but one where you could choose from a number of routes, always emerging eventually at the central staircase.

It is simply a highly pleasurable and well-organized building, especially where its scale is concerned. It is a pleasing size; you can go around it and see everything in the space of an hour and a half. The only complaint was that it was just a little too small to properly display the permanent collection. And now the floor space is 40 per cent larger, thanks not only to the new building but also to additional space in the old, with the stripping out of the auditorium and additional exhibition space created in the “rooms behind the scenes”. This also had beneficial effects for the routing. We decided that everything not used for exhibition purposes should be removed from the old building and brought together in the entrance hall below the “bathtub”, so that the whole of Weissman’s building has the function of a museum.

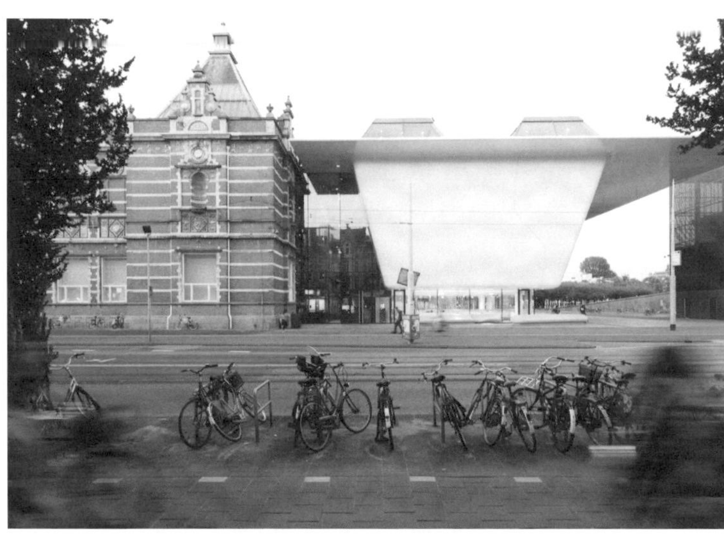

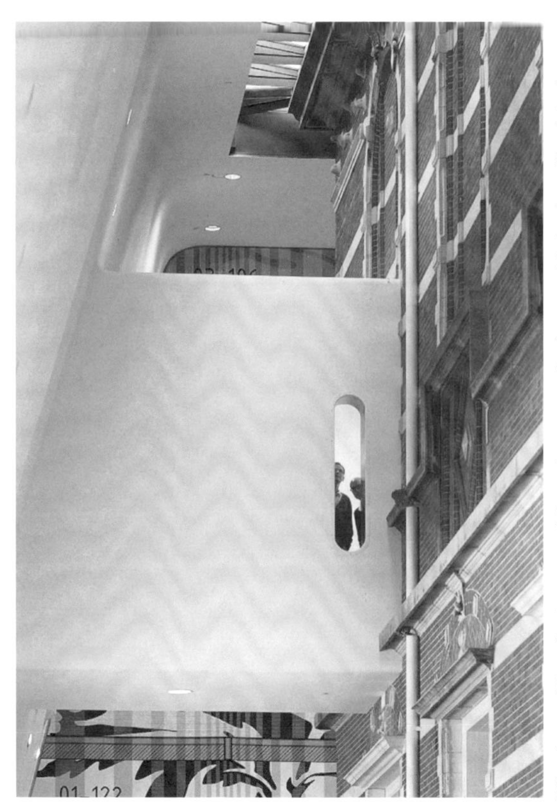

The transition between old and new, exterior and interior. “Inside however, our use of precisely the same treatment for the rooms means that you are hardly aware that you are moving from the old into the new, except perhaps if you look out of one of the small windows which we have made in the pedestrian walkways.”

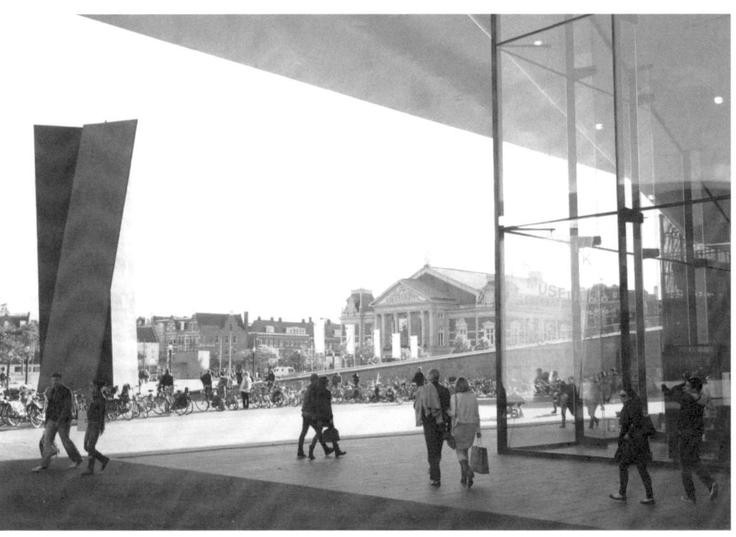
The square in front of the museum entrance. "A side benefit is that the canopy provides a partly covered courtyard which can be used in a number of ways."

The new escalator in its yellow shaft was added to improve circulation, allowing movement directly from the first floor in the new building to the sub-basement. This makes it possible to stage a continuous exhibition, with visitors remaining within the ambience of the art on display as they pass, all unawares, through the central hall. Having purchased your ticket you can view the art without the disturbing feeling that the building is getting in your way.

The exterior of the new building may look pretty spectacular, but at the same time it is based on functional logic. The use of a giant canopy is primarily intended to shield the ground floor from the sun. The building faces south and we wanted to keep the first floor open, uniting the interior and exterior. So it was essential to ensure that the interior didn't become overheated. A side benefit is that the canopy provides a partly covered courtyard that can be used in a number of ways and where visitors can shelter to queue during rain. The canopy makes the location of the entrance immediately obvious. The reason that the walls below the canopy slope while the internal partitions are vertical is that all the air conditioning ducts run between them, and access is required for maintenance. So although it may look like an aircraft, the form originally arose from functional considerations, although ultimately it does of course have an aesthetic significance. So, I feel that on the one hand we have created a highly expressive building, and on the other hand the new entrance has given a new orientation not only to the Stedelijk Museum itself but also to the Van Gogh Museum, the Rijksmuseum and the Concertgebouw. The urban planning aspects of the solution were a real discovery. The brief called for the relocation of the entrance to the Van Baerlestraat, which we felt was only a partial answer.

Our design melded together the old and new on the first floor so that the new rooms blend in completely with the existing building and use the same logistics. Then below the entrance area comes a completely new part. There is no daylight here, but that doesn't matter quite so much now that artificial light is so good, and it allows the space to be used in all kinds of ways, for

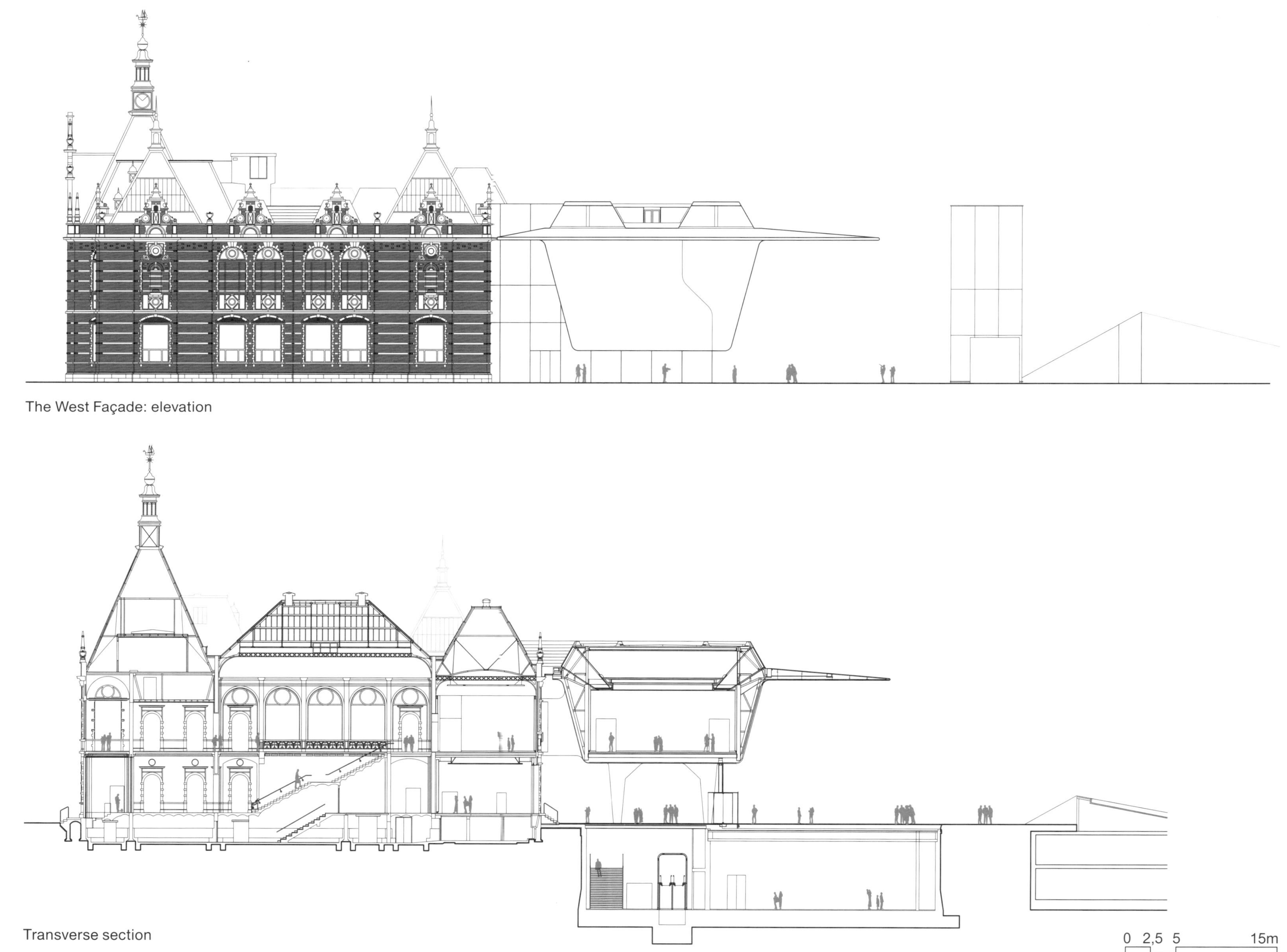

The West Façade: elevation

Transverse section

example for video installations. If this enormous space had been set down on the Museumplein it would have closed everything in, right up to the so-called "dog-ear". The program was so extensive that without a basement it would have filled up the entire site, two floors high. But by placing a major element below ground and raising another element aloft we have succeeded in increasing rather than decreasing the size of the Museumplein. I don't mind saying this was a tremendous trick to pull off. The open space runs in through the entrance right to the rear façade of the old building, which now stands, fully restored, separated from the new. The result is a balancing act between the old and new, blended together on the upper floor, and separated at ground level."

To what extent do the spaces dictate the way in which the museum can be used for exhibitions?

"There's not a great deal of controversy about the exhibition of art and how that can be done in older and newer buildings. What is nice is that not all museums are the same, and also that time and the construction of the museum have roles to play. That means that you are sometimes faced with rooms that are a little more detailed than anonymous white spaces. This can mean that curators and artists are required to respond to the building. We have, of course, attempted to retain the tranquility of the original Stedelijk Museum, and to make the light on the upper level of the old building even better than it was, despite the restriction that, according to today's museum standards, only half of the previous amount of light should be allowed in. Despite this, with the new filters it certainly looks at least as light as before. The rooms are now whiter, brighter and larger than they were. First, we installed a new floor. There was a lot of discussion about this, as for many people that creaky herringbone floor of the old building really summed up the Stedelijk Museum: a parquet floor with heating grilles in the middle. I too grew up with that floor, but Gijs van Tuyl was very clear about it: there would have to be a new floor. In his view the old floor was too obtrusive and imposed unnecessary restrictions. Too much about the Stedelijk Museum itself he said, and not good for the art. So, a quieter, more level floor has been provided. The new floor is quite a bit lighter than what it replaced.

Secondly, we increased the height of the rooms. A sun screen used to hang at the level where the rounded coving begins, but we have reduced the size of this filter and suspended it separately from the walls. It now hangs nearly a meter higher, so that the rooms appear more spacious, while in reality the floor area is a little smaller with the installation of the air ducts within the cavity walls. These walls have been rounded off a little at the top, to avoid the stereotypical gallery wall look. The light now reflects from the upper surface of the screen back onto the curved coping, beautifully softening the high space. The elevated filter also allows one to view more of the old building. By making the rooms whiter, and by changing the color in the corridors from a

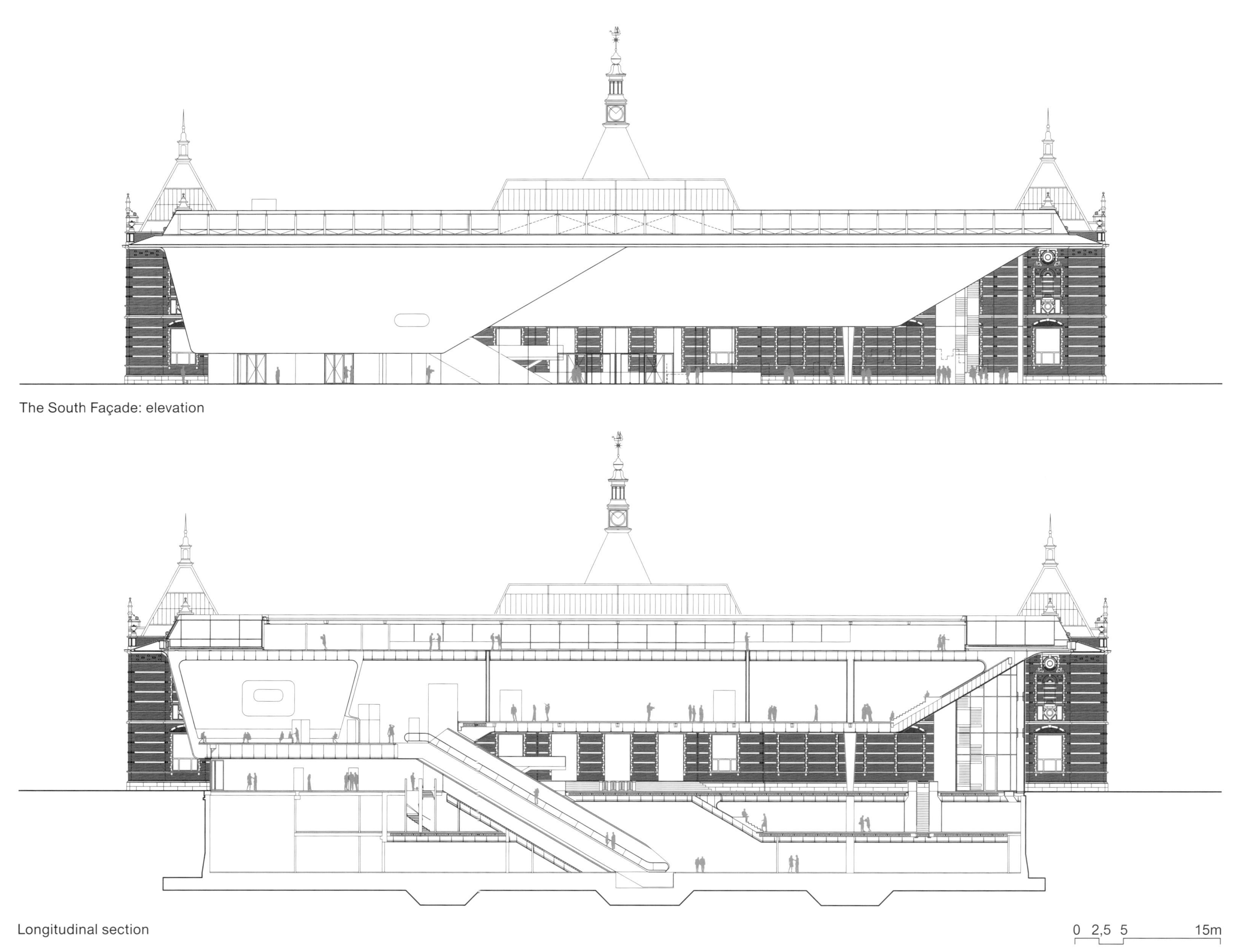

The South Façade: elevation

Longitudinal section

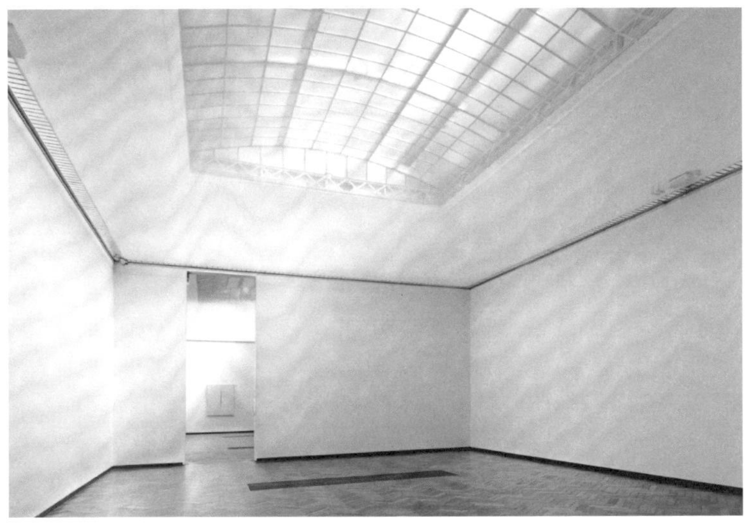

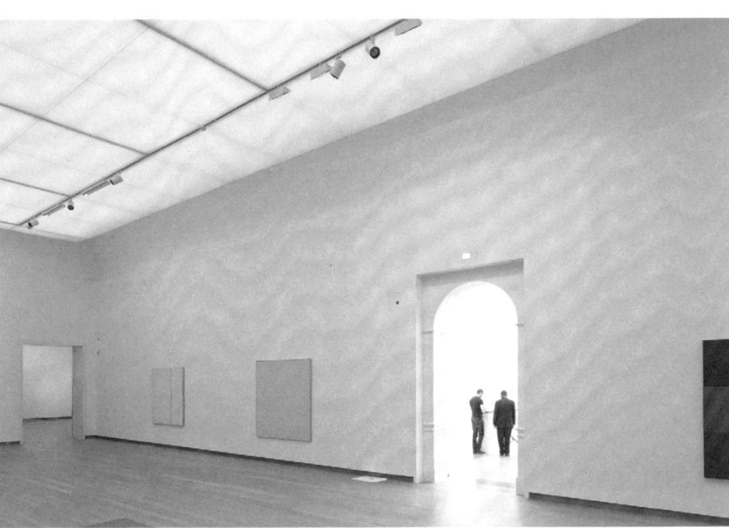

The old sun screen and the new light filter in the IMC Gallery today. "Sunscreening formerly hung at the level where the rounded coving begins, but we have reduced the size of this filter and suspended it separately from the walls. It is now nearly a metre higher, giving a greater impression of space."

woody brown to white, we have also pulled off another balancing act. On the one hand the museum rooms have been modernized, on the other hand we have allowed more of the older building to be seen. Apart from that we have concealed not only the light fittings but also the sockets at the base of the walls, which are now invisible above the set-back skirting. The result is what we might call a proper building, rather than just a bare, white space."

Did you put more time and energy into the renovation than the new wing?

"No, because once you have the theoretical solution, it is just a matter of working things out in reality. And besides, as you can see from photographs taken when everything was stripped out, it is a fairly simple building. I think the new-build work took more time in the end, what with the basement, the steel structure and the façade."

Does the finished building deviate from the original plans?

"If you look now at the first drawings made during the tendering process, the whole thing is already there. There were some changes to the location and size of certain rooms in areas not open to the public, and also the entrance area was dealt with a little differently. That was in part because the director, Gijs van Tuyl, had quite firm views about this area: his idea was that as soon as possible after entering the building you should feel you are in a museum and should be seeing works of art. We still used room with the Karel Appel mural as an extension to the entrance area, with an information desk and cloakroom facilities, as we felt that this was a room with many passageways. There is not much opportunity to hang anything here, particularly since two walls were already occupied by artworks. Gijs van Tuyl wanted a sculpture gallery there, while our thought was that this could make the entrance rather narrow. If further changes are needed this could still be done. So if visitor numbers are higher than anticipated, the boundary between the paid and unpaid areas can be relocated."

Tickets could also be sold outside the building, as at Jean Nouvel's Musée Quai Branly in Paris.

"They have also done that at the Neues Museum in Berlin, because it is so busy there. They have brought in a couple of containers to house the ticket counters. The Stedelijk Museum could bring in a container and position it beside the lift if it is very busy in the early months.

Our original proposal had the cloakrooms in the basement, as was previously the case at the Boijmans van Beuningen Museum in Rotterdam, where you could get away from the hustle and bustle to take off your coat and use the restroom.

We actually proposed escalators to take you down there, and that would have dealt with a lot of the congestion problems around the entrance. But Gijs van Tuyl didn't feel this was sufficiently visitor-friendly. So, in the end there is one cloakroom behind the cash desk, with another area available next to the stairs if it gets very busy. We also looked at electrical systems of the type they have at the MoMA in New York, but if these ever break down there could be a lot of trouble so we didn't risk it.

Apart from relatively minor matters like these, little was changed. I was gratified by the way the clients continued to stand behind the design: the contract client was the City of Amsterdam, of course, but the Stedelijk Museum also had plenty of say. Even

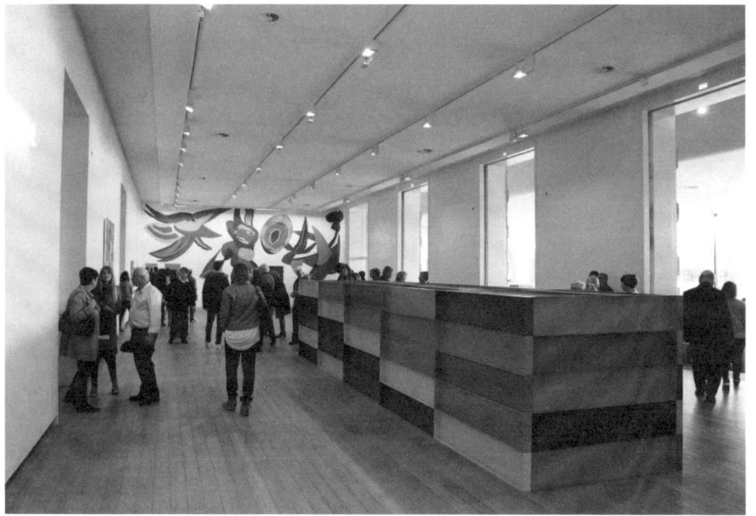

The Audi Gallery, with the mural by Karel Appel and *Untitled* by Donald Judd. "We still used the Karel Appel room as an extension to the entrance area."

when things got a bit tense and savings had to be made, they continued to offer support, and they let that be known outside too."

What was scrapped because of cuts?

"There was going to be computer-controlled lighting in the ceiling of the basement, allowing you to imitate daylight and produce all kinds of effects, but that fell victim to cuts. However, it could still be installed later. That was our approach to savings throughout: the basics would be right, and anything that was dropped for the sake of savings could still be added later. The first thing to be dropped was the balcony in the auditorium. We had thought about a section of the auditorium façade that would open to create a balcony, like an airplane door-cum-stairs. This would have been a nice extra, but it was also a logical part to economize."

Is it a satisfying feeling to have succeeded where a succession of designers before you have failed?

"That's not how we look at it. It gives me a very satisfied feeling that with my background (after all I pretty much grew up in the Stedelijk Museum) we, the office, have been able to make this happen. Of course, they would have had to build to that design by Venturi Scott Brown. That was a lot bigger than what we have built, and they would have been finished far earlier."

Logistics seem to have become increasingly important in museum architecture, with larger visitor streams. To what extent did this affect the design?

"It certainly had some effect. The new Stedelijk Museum can easily handle five or six hundred thousand visitors a year. This is a very different picture to the Anne Frank House, which we also renovated and expanded. They have to get a million people a year through a small building that is totally unsuitable for use as a museum. When you compare the dimensions with the Rijksmuseum and the Van Gogh and look at the visitor numbers, it should work. It's not just about the people, but also about the number of coats in the cloakroom and the size of the catering facilities. In any case, what we have done is to design a building that can be used flexibly. That includes the museum shop, which is laid out like a supermarket, not fixed to the floor. If it turns out that the shop is too large or too small it can be changed at will."

Are these things you have learned through designing airports?

"Yes, and railway stations. Logistics is important there, as it is in museums. We enjoy this kind of work, solving that kind of problem. One thing that hasn't really been resolved at the Stedelijk Museum is that it doesn't have what you might call a "service side". There's no side or back to the building. So that's why you have the separate lift. This has the advantage that it partially hides the loading and unloading activities at the adjacent supermarket, but delivering items to the museum continues to be a complicated matter.

Artworks and some of the other goods come in via the lift, but the kitchen waste has to go out through the service entrance, which requires discipline if the whole thing isn't to descend into a mess. But everyone is aware of this; we made it quite clear at the outset. You can't have everything."

Will the new Stedelijk Museum have effects on the functioning of the Museumplein?

"You can see this already. We see now that there are a number of museum directors at these museums bordering the square who plan things together, and there are plans for more activities on the Museumplein in future. We can also see that the route from the Stedelijk Museum to the Rijksmuseum has taken on more significance, and that Kisho Kurokawa's extension to the Van Gogh Museum is working better now that the route between the extension and the museum itself is being used more intensively. The Van Gogh Museum is also exploring the possibility of a second entrance on that side."

And the "dog's ear"?

"It was always said that the "dog's ear" was an obstruction. Our plan is unlike any other, because we have come up with a solution. I would prefer it though if the dog's ear were gone. Michael van Gessel and Ton Schaap have been drawing up new plans for the Museumplein, without the dog's ear, but they are too expensive to implement at present. We have also produced drawings for a supermarket a little further along, below the Museumplein, but that isn't going to happen in the next decade or two. So yes, you could say that it's a pity that the dog's ear is still in the way, but there isn't any alternative. My feeling is that the square in front of the entrance could be something similar to the square in front of the Pompidou Centre but on a smaller scale. It is a lovely south-facing location, so why not a bit of everything there, with activities initiated by the museum and also people selling things, people using it to sit?"

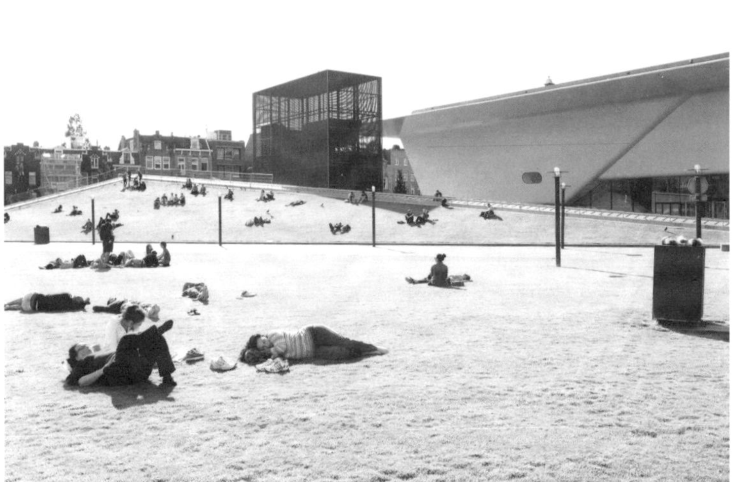

The Museumplein as laid out by Sven-Ingvar Andersson, with the "dog's ear".

Does innovation play a role in museum architecture?

"Yes: education now plays a greater role for all cultural buildings, so that means you need more spaces—spaces that are more than just museum rooms. Media art is also more important today, and that means more demand for darker rooms. And there has been a lot of change where lighting is concerned. Lighting continues to be very important for paintings, sculpture and installations: there has of course been a great deal of technical innovation in that field, so we now have blinds up in the roof, with a filter system above that and artificial light below—three times as many options when it comes to coordinating the lighting of the rooms."

And what about innovations in the area of typology?

"There isn't a single type of art museum. You might think a gigantic black box you could put anything in would be ideal, but it isn't. Much art is tied to a specific location, so what we have attempted to do is to achieve as much variation in the building as possible, within the constraints of its simple layout. This is also one of the charms of the old Stedelijk Museum, that it housed different types of rooms. There's that big space in the middle, around the staircase; large halls with a distinction between those at the corners and those in between; rectangular display cabinets downstairs, while those upstairs have a sort of diorama feel about them. Despite the fact that it is a very simple, symmetrical building it is still highly diverse and individual. We have attempted to connect the new hall symmetrically with the old Hall of Honor while bringing the overhead lighting in a different way as well as providing another exhibition space alongside, slightly asymmetrically.

The new exhibition space below is very different, and on the way there you pass by the mezzanine floor near the auditorium with its variations in level and orientation. This has resulted in a proper route through the building, and one which is never tedious. The building remains a single structure because of the use of the same materials throughout.

There is also more room for debate, calling for rooms where people can sit, with tiered seating. Spaces like this can be used to display videos or for lectures. Parties will be held within the museum in connection with sponsorship; there will also be more receptions. The old and new buildings are ideal for these purposes. Around the staircase in the old building and above and below the auditorium is a nice transitional area before one enters the large hall.

These things have nothing to do with art, though. Where the display of art is concerned, the dimensions of the rooms are significant. Contemporary art often features relatively large works of course, and to cater to this we have created an enormous room below: this is really completely different from what was there before, and different from to what is typical in museums.

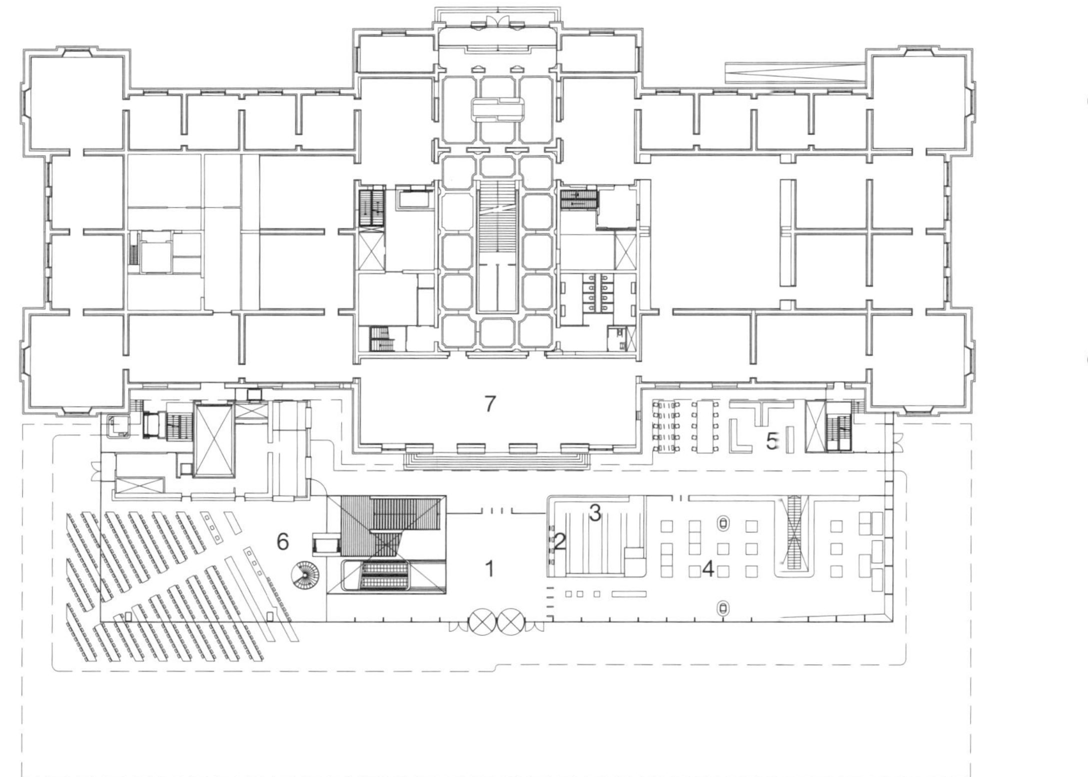

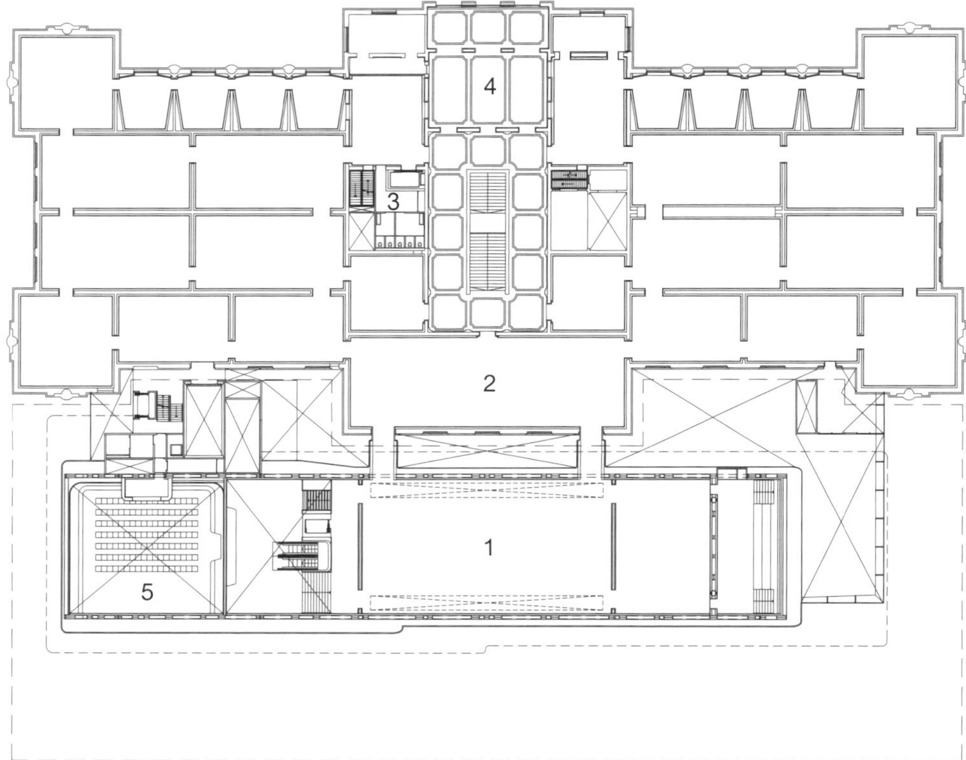

Ground floor

1 Entrance
2 Tickets
3 Cloakroom
4 Shop
5 Information
6 Restaurant
7 Exhibition space, old building: Audi Gallery

Top floor

1 Exhibition space, new building: VandenEnde Foundation Gallery
2 Exhibition space, old building: IMC Gallery
3 Toilets
4 Café
5 Teijin auditorium

We have not stuck strictly to the program in this case. We designed the large lower room in such a way that a number of smaller spaces can be fitted into it, and we created fewer new rooms with side lighting than originally requested. Our thinking was that there are already plenty of those at the Stedelijk, it would be better to make something it doesn't already have. We did take a risk there where the competition was concerned, just as we did when we completely reversed the building. That hadn't been requested either. Failing to provide precisely what is requested can lead to immediate rejection from the competition, but in this case the jury were open to variations. Gijs van Tuyl was appointed as director the day after the jury announced its decision. He was shown the various plans without being told who had won, and immediately said ours was the best. That was really great for us."

How long can the Stedelijk Museum continue to function as a museum building now?

"Just as long as the old building. Our solution with the spaces means they could carry on for another hundred years. It won't actually last that long, because the pace of change is always accelerating, but it will stand for fifty years, that's for sure. It is also intriguing to note that, before it closed, the old building housed expensive artworks without any climate control for nearly a century, while the demands of the insurers and the strict requirements of those lending works mean that this is no longer permissible. 40 per cent of the budget for the extension was spent on technical installations, while at the same time doubts were being raised about whether this was all really so good for the artworks. After all, this art hung in the museum for a hundred years in a standard living-room climate, just like most art in the world."

There was a long period between the design of the building and its eventual completion. How did that affect the process?

"During the building process we dealt with two different museum directors, two or three different people at the local authority, and three or four different construction managers. What you need to keep in mind during such a lengthy process is that you make a building like this for the city and for the artworks, not for the current director or alderperson or manager. It is always the problem with these projects—you need to have the nerve to just carry on with what you believe is right. It's great when your clients allow you to do that, and when they are pleased with the result. And that has been quite unusual with this building, the way everyone stood behind us all the way."

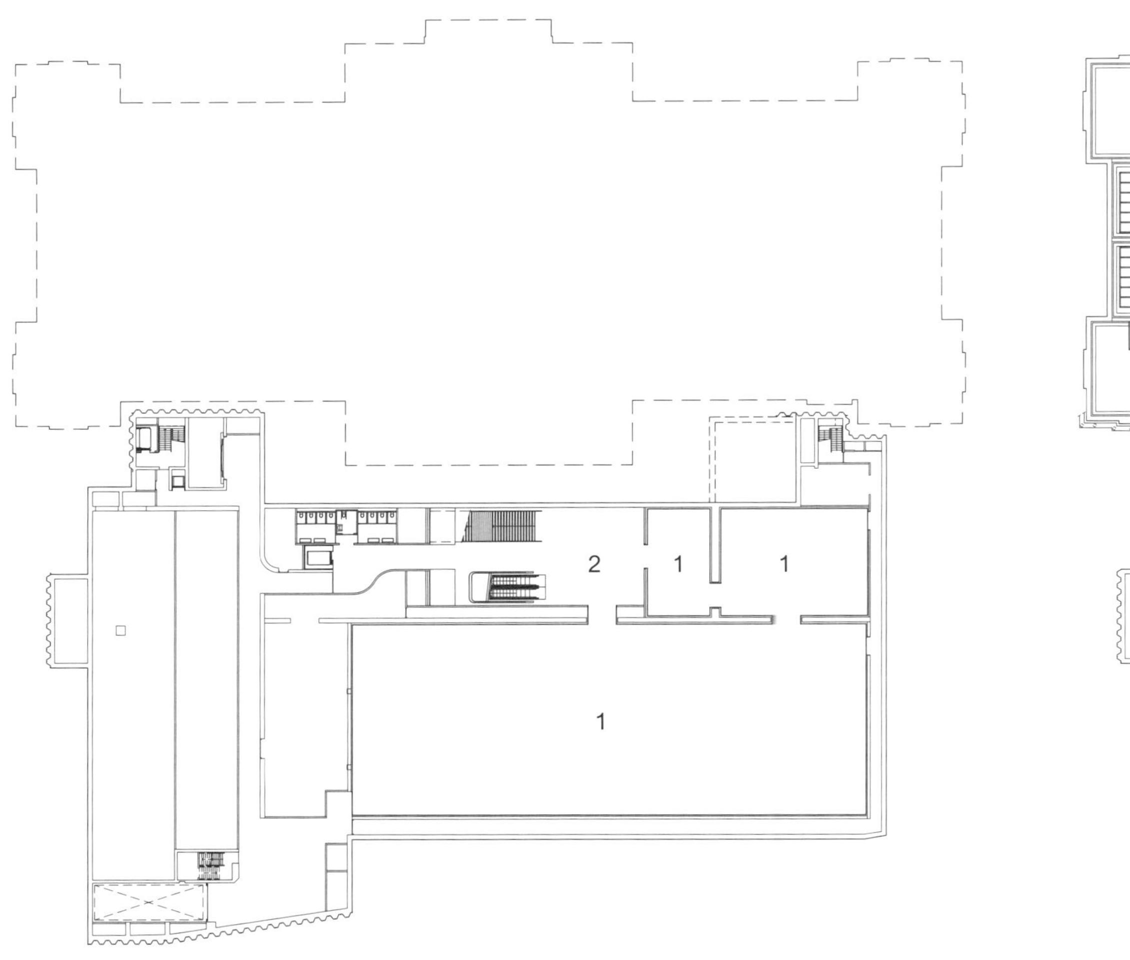

Lower floor –2

1 Exhibition space, new building: ABN AMRO Gallery
2 Hall

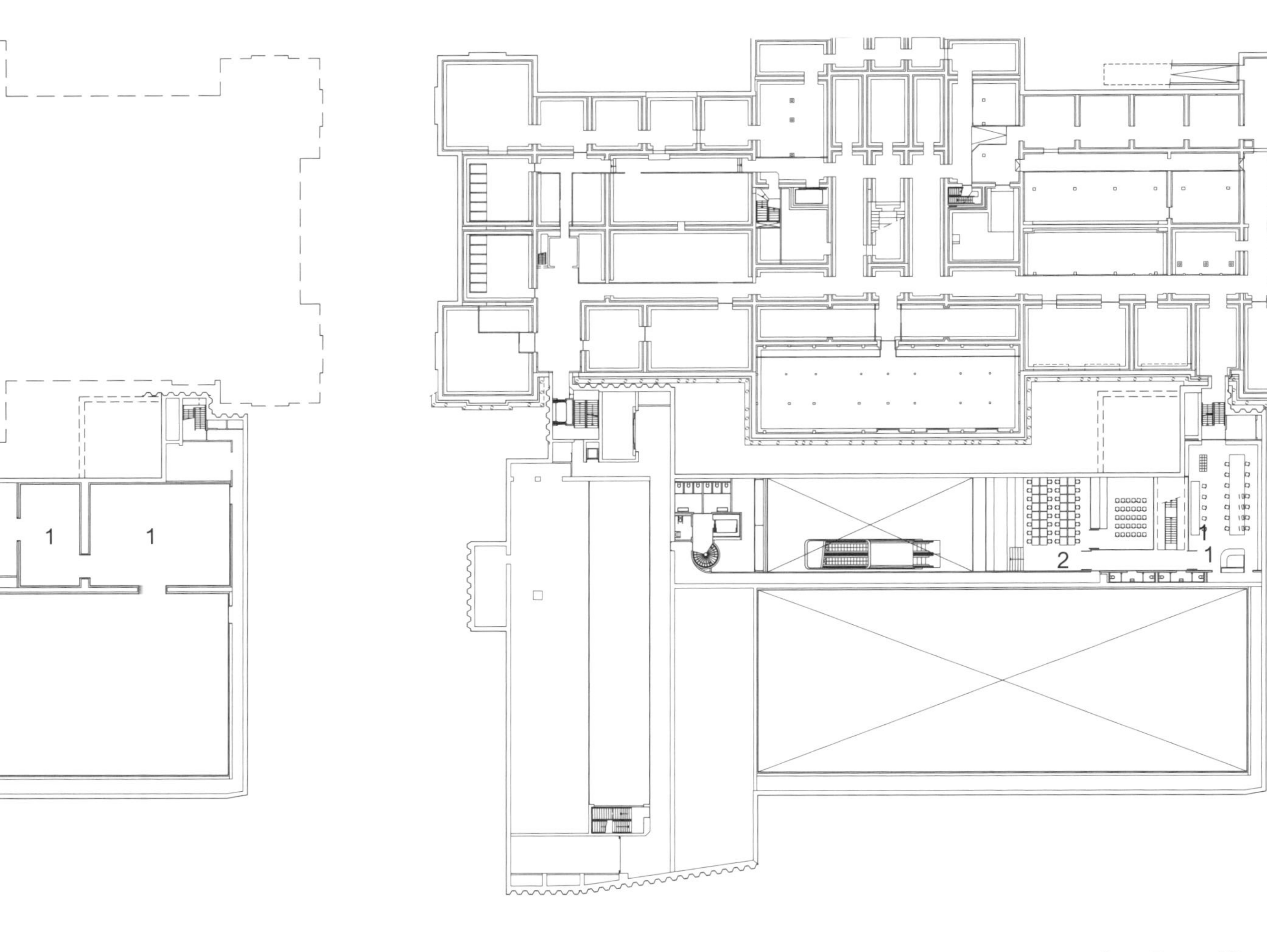

Lower floor –1

1 Reading Room
2 Education Room

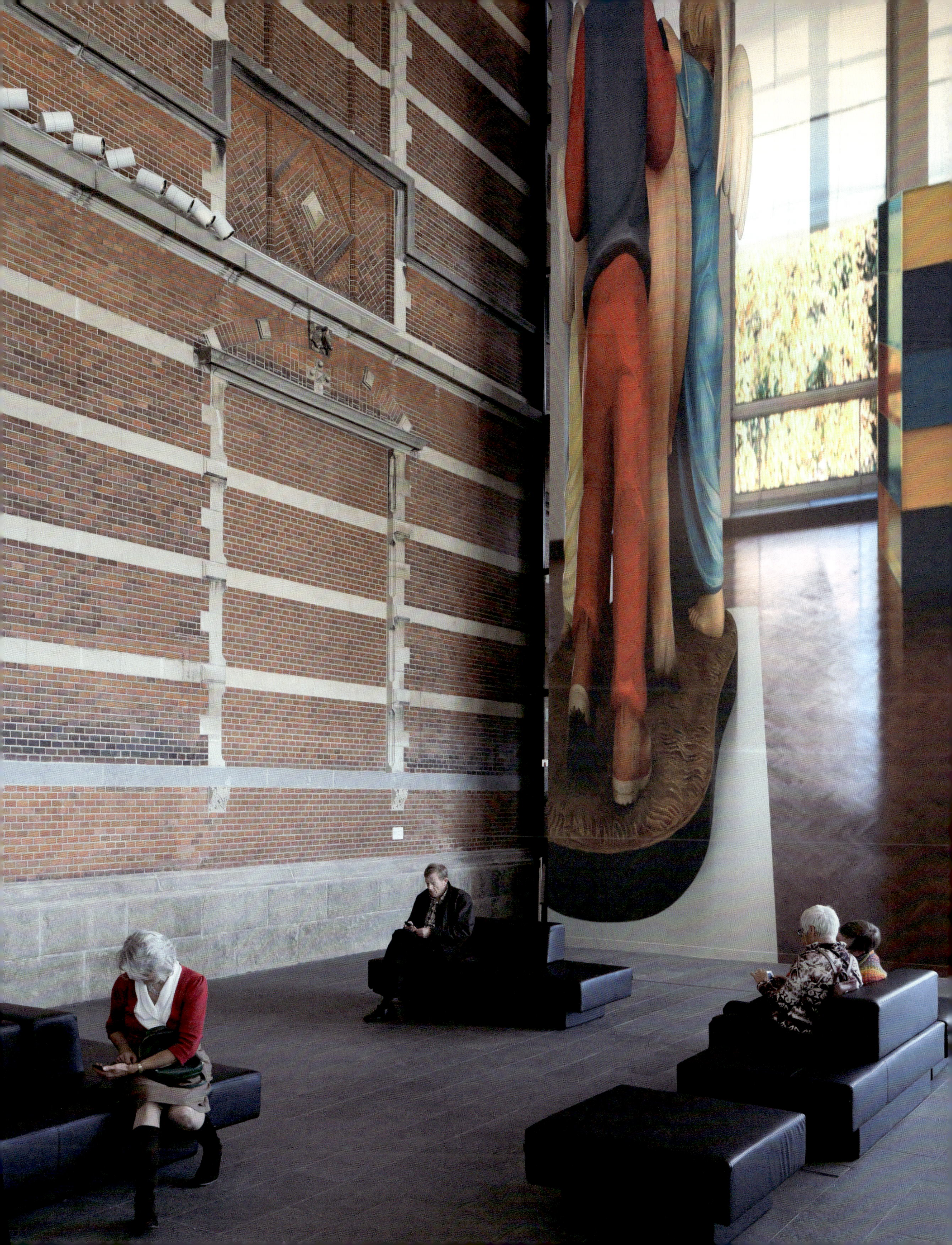

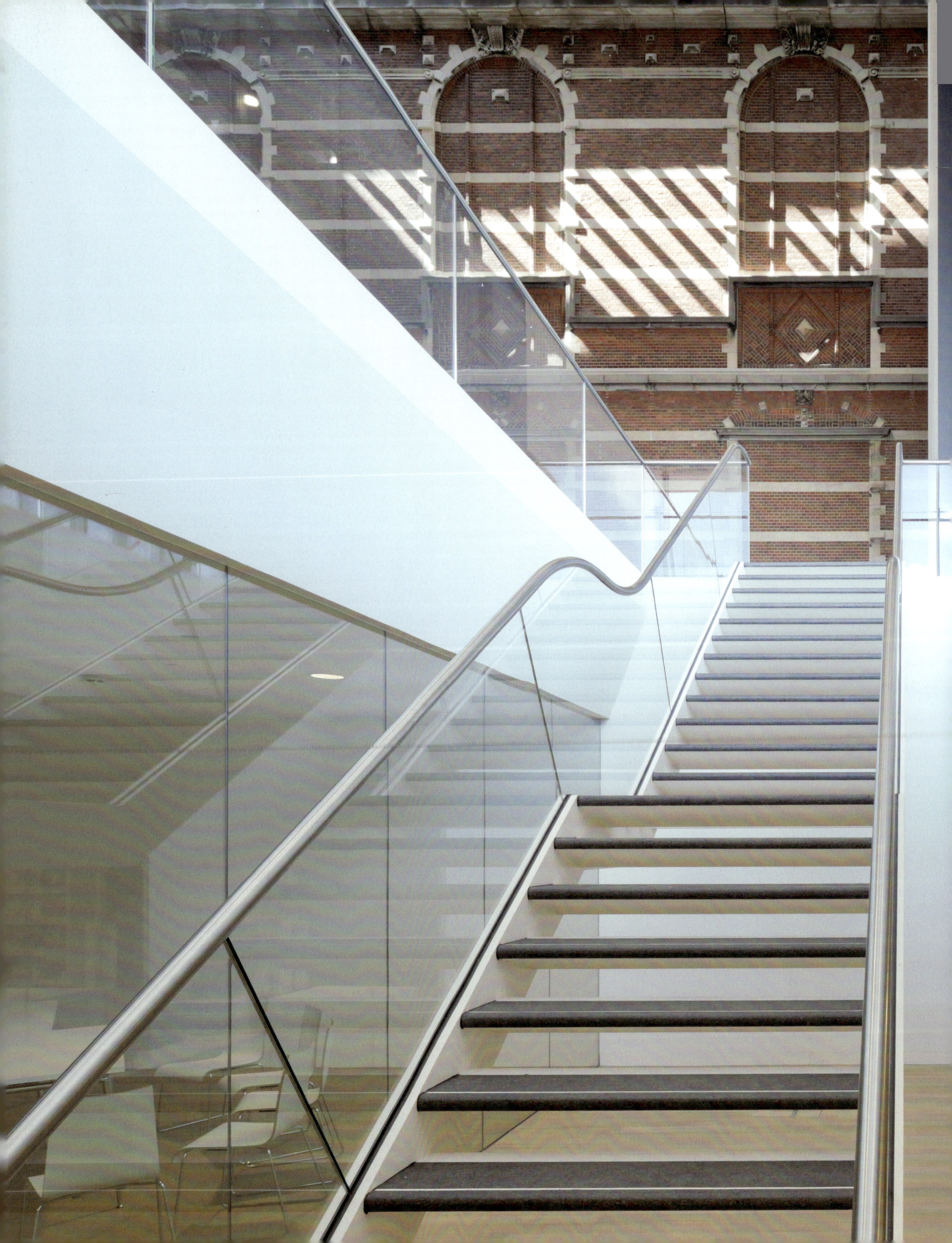

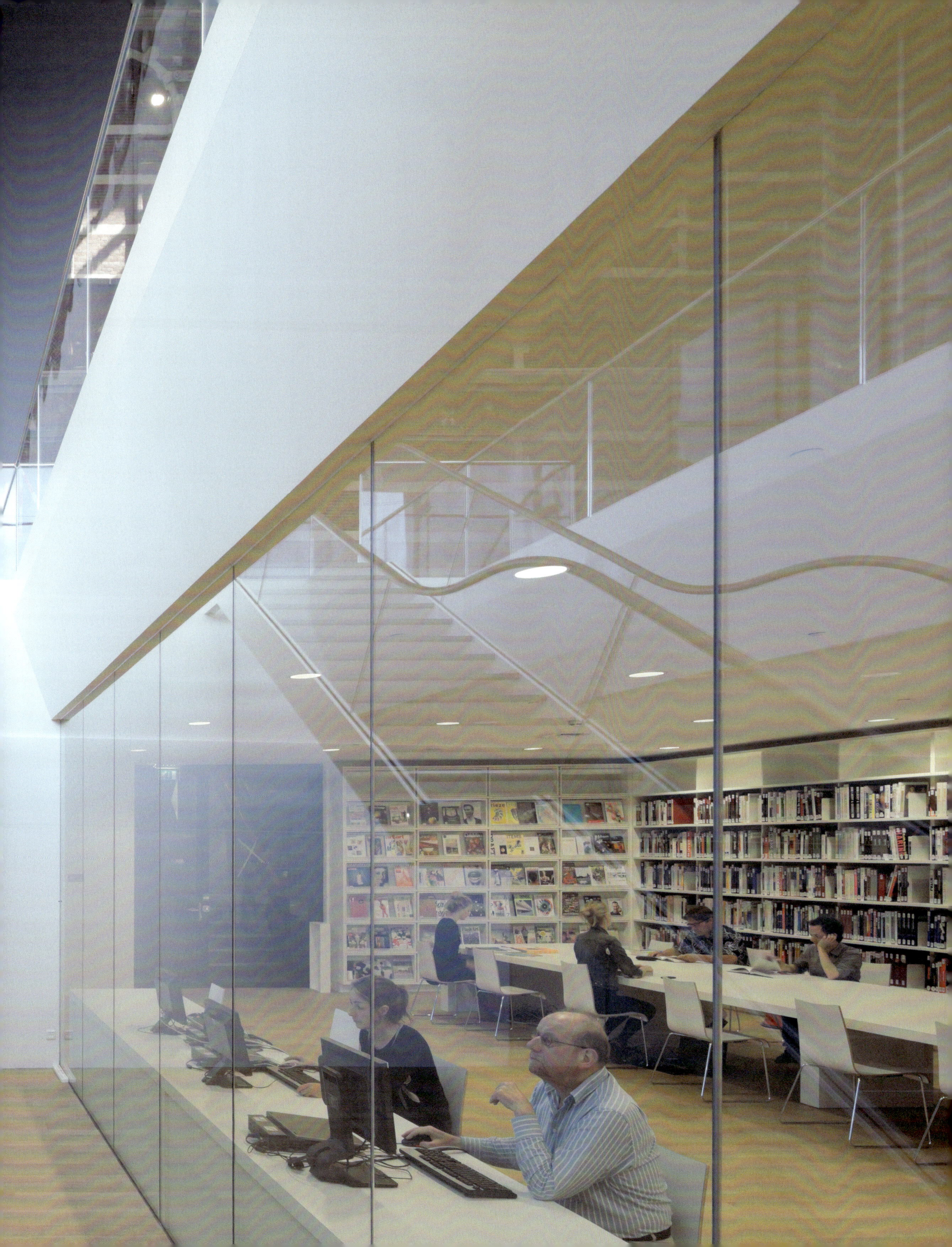

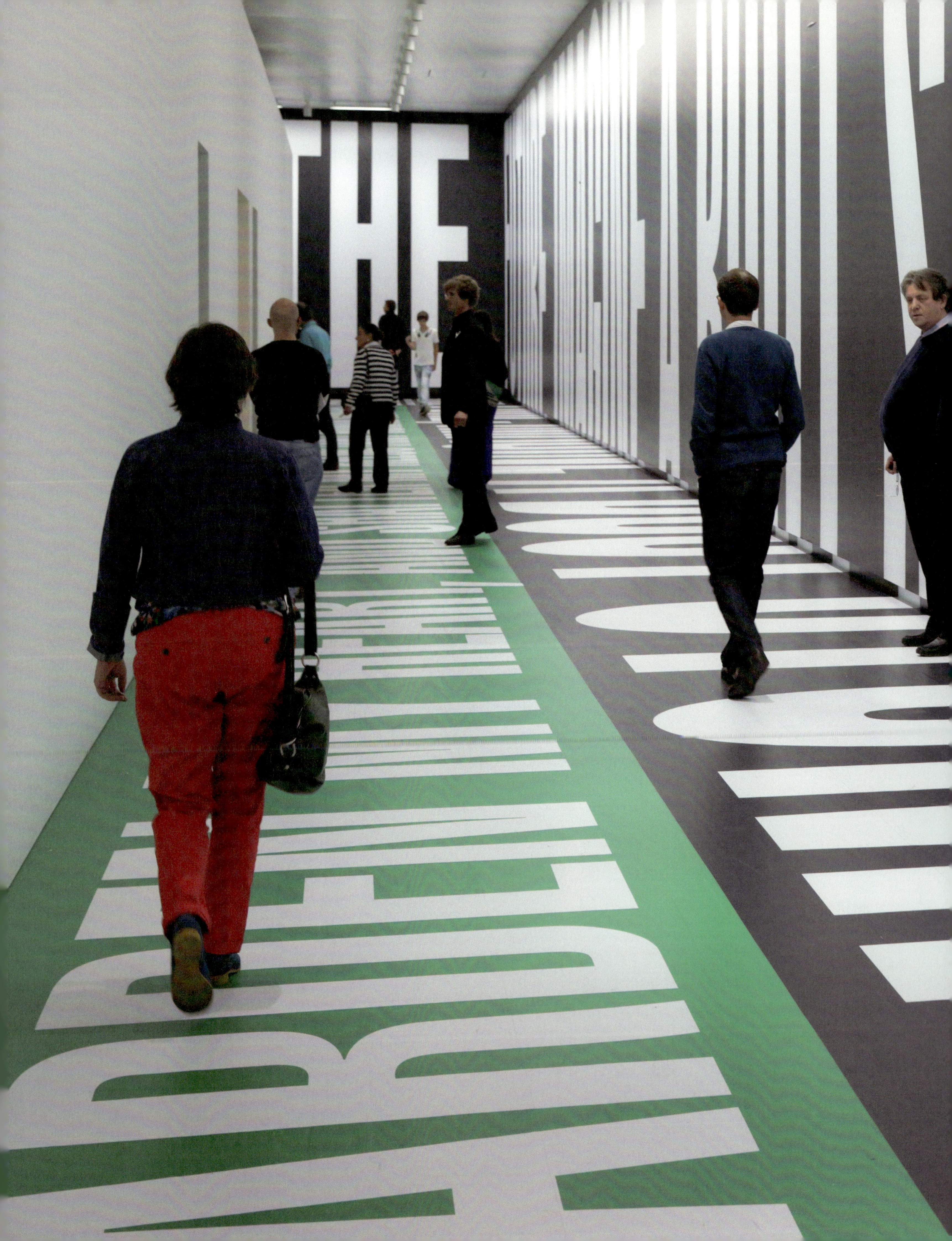
THE

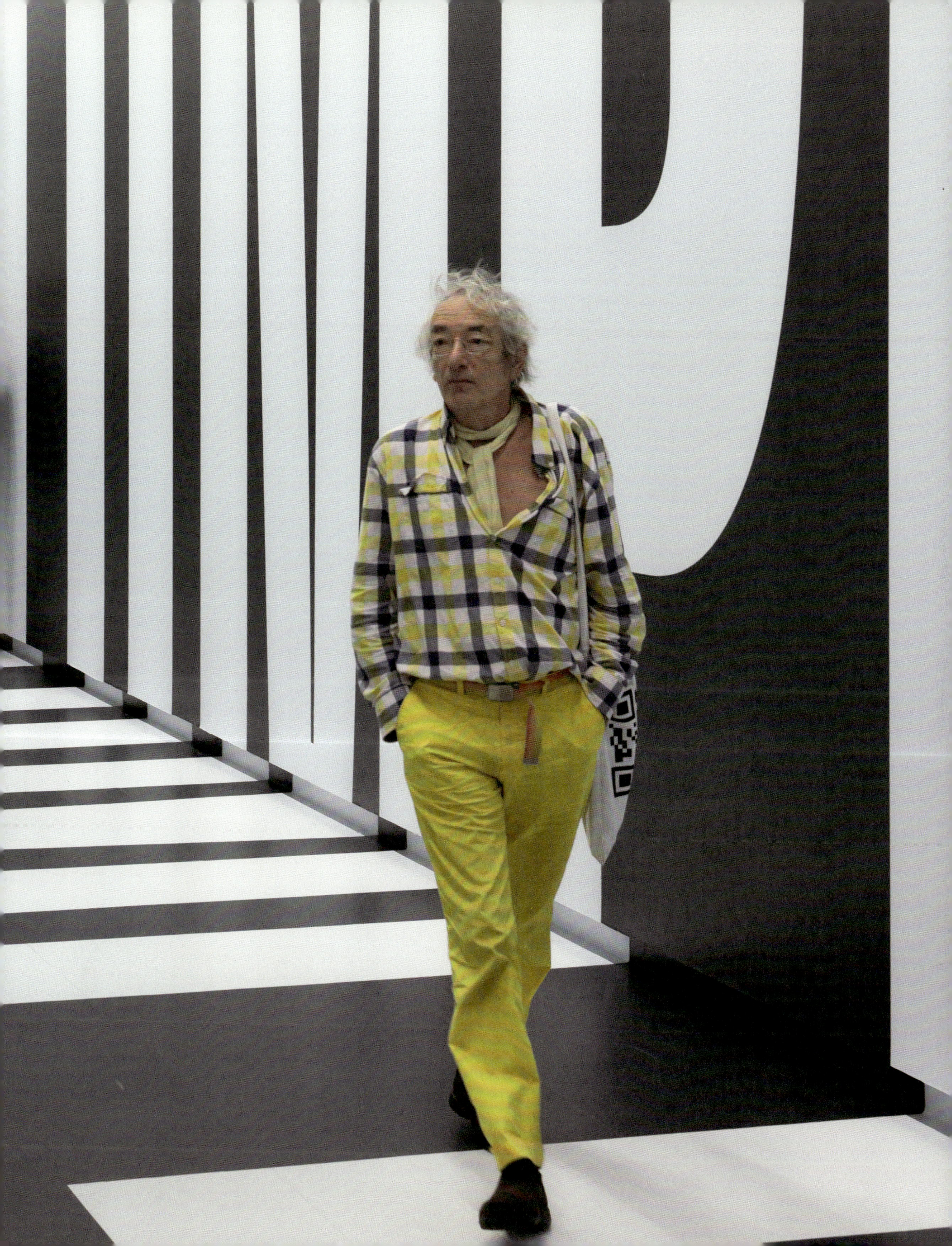

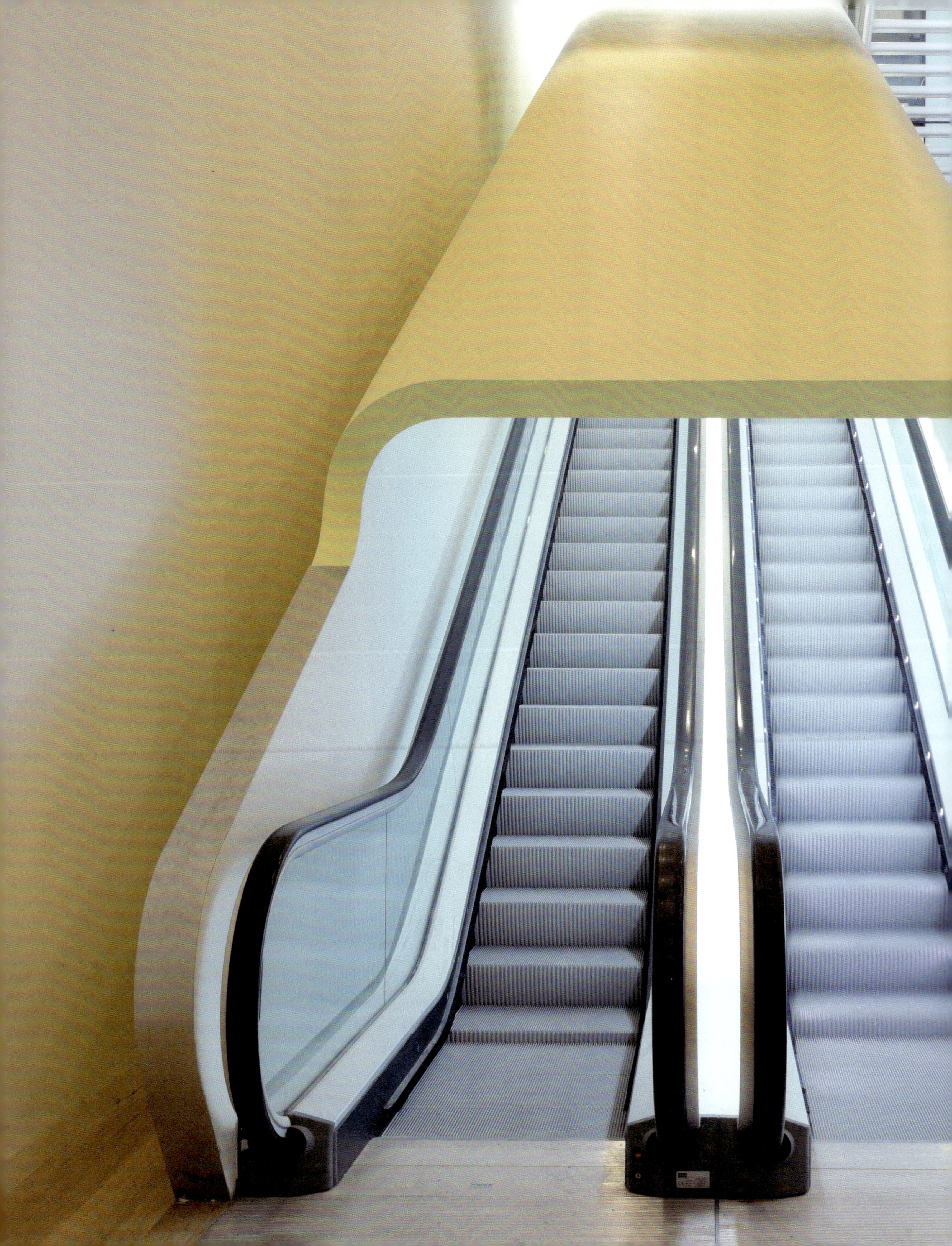

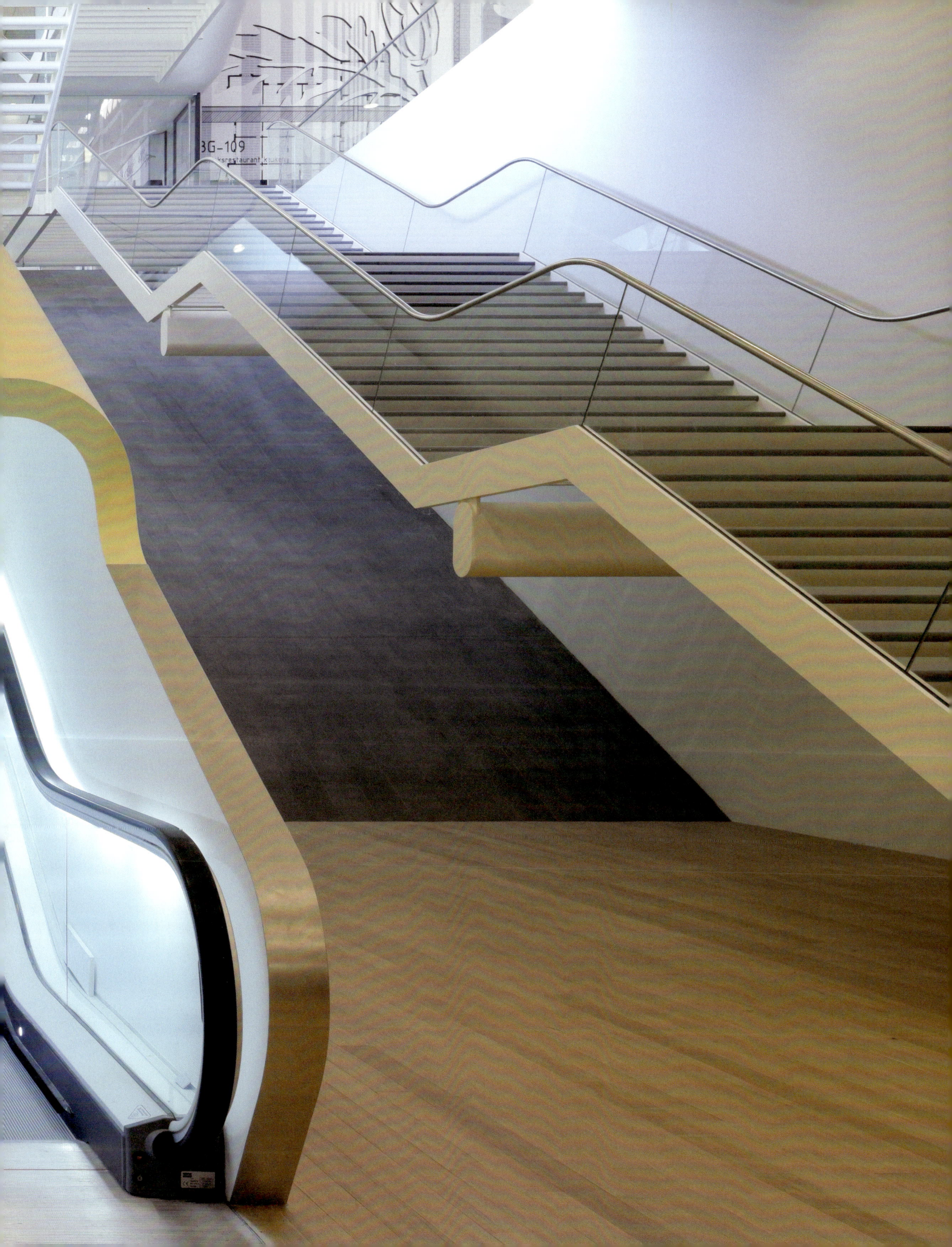
BG-109

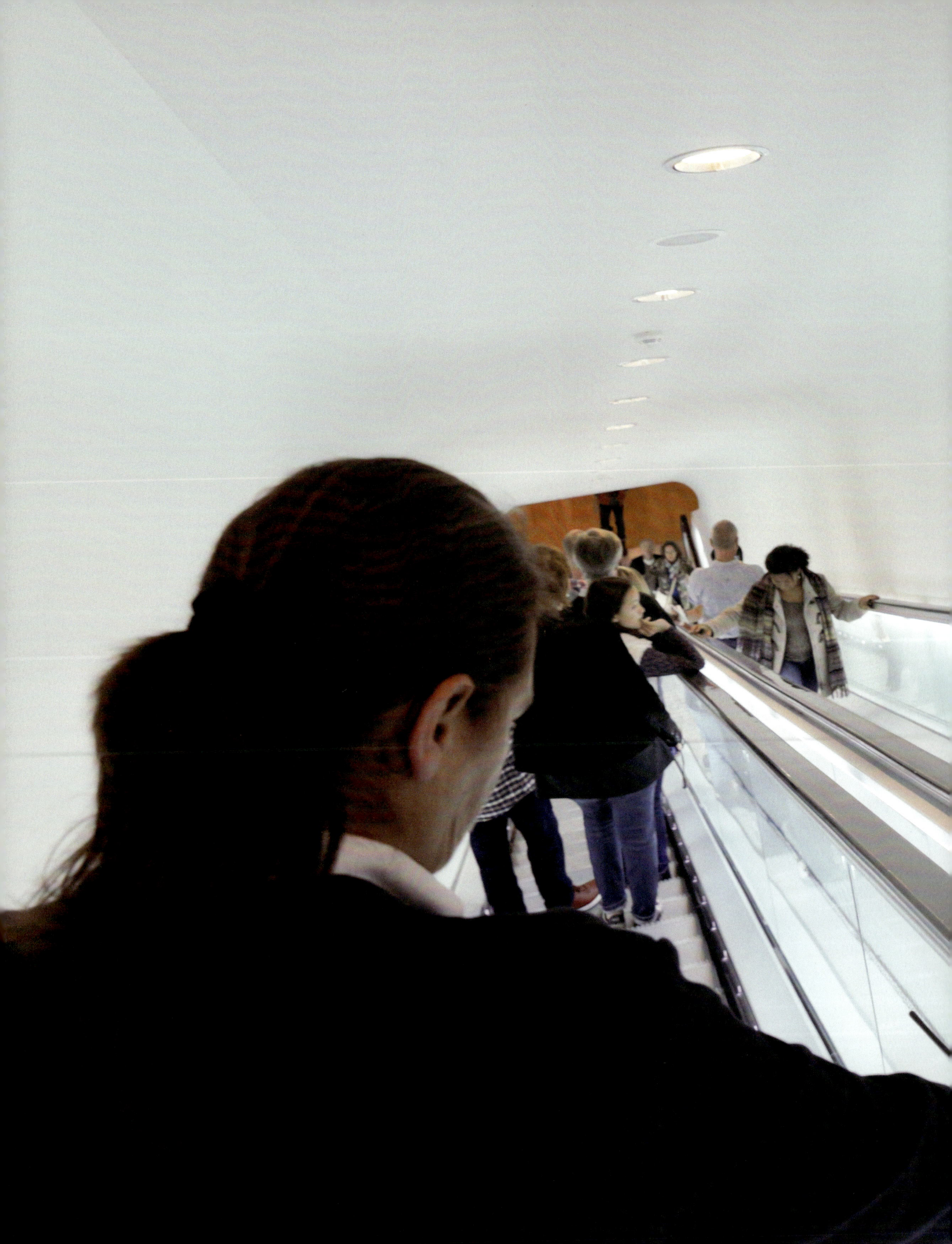

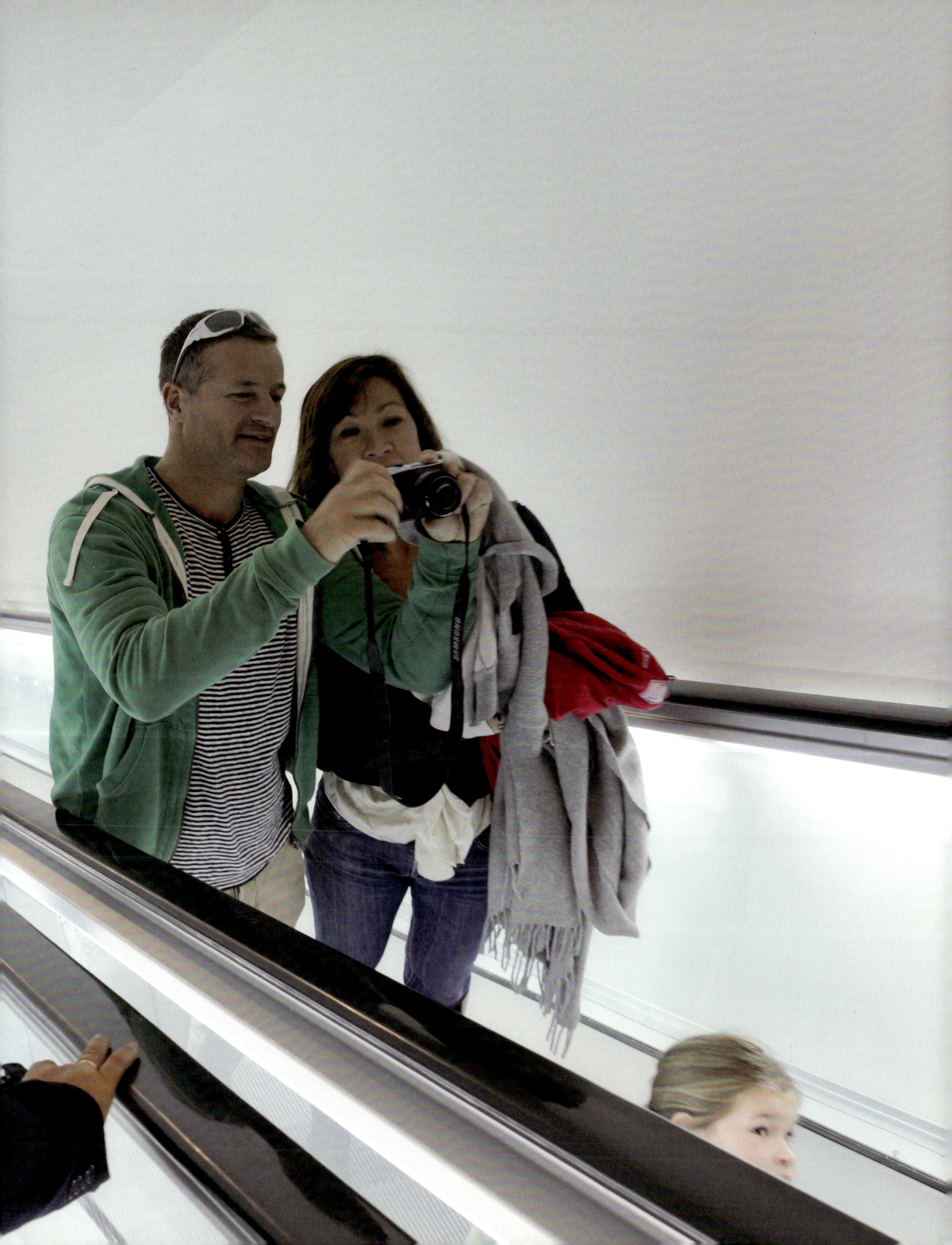

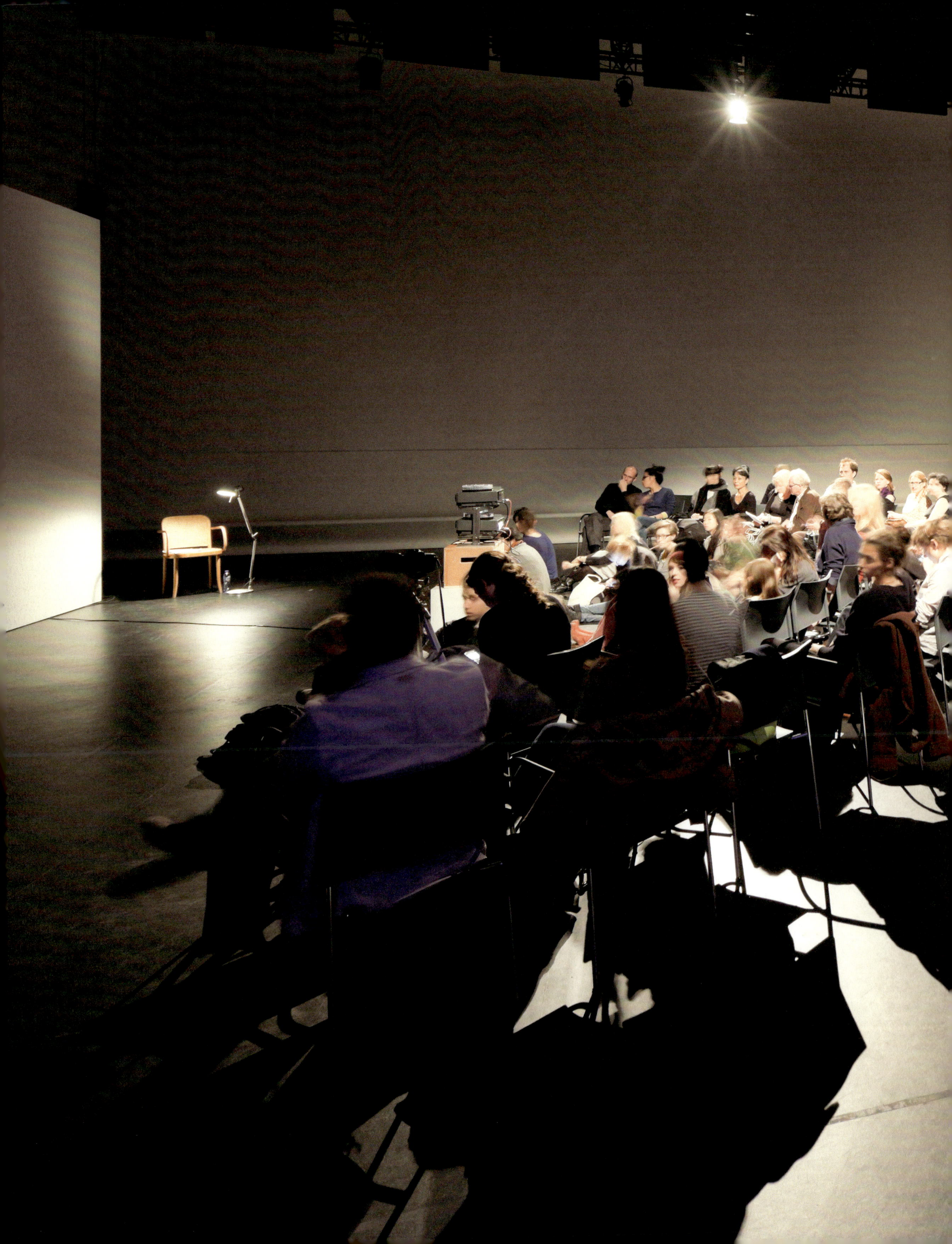

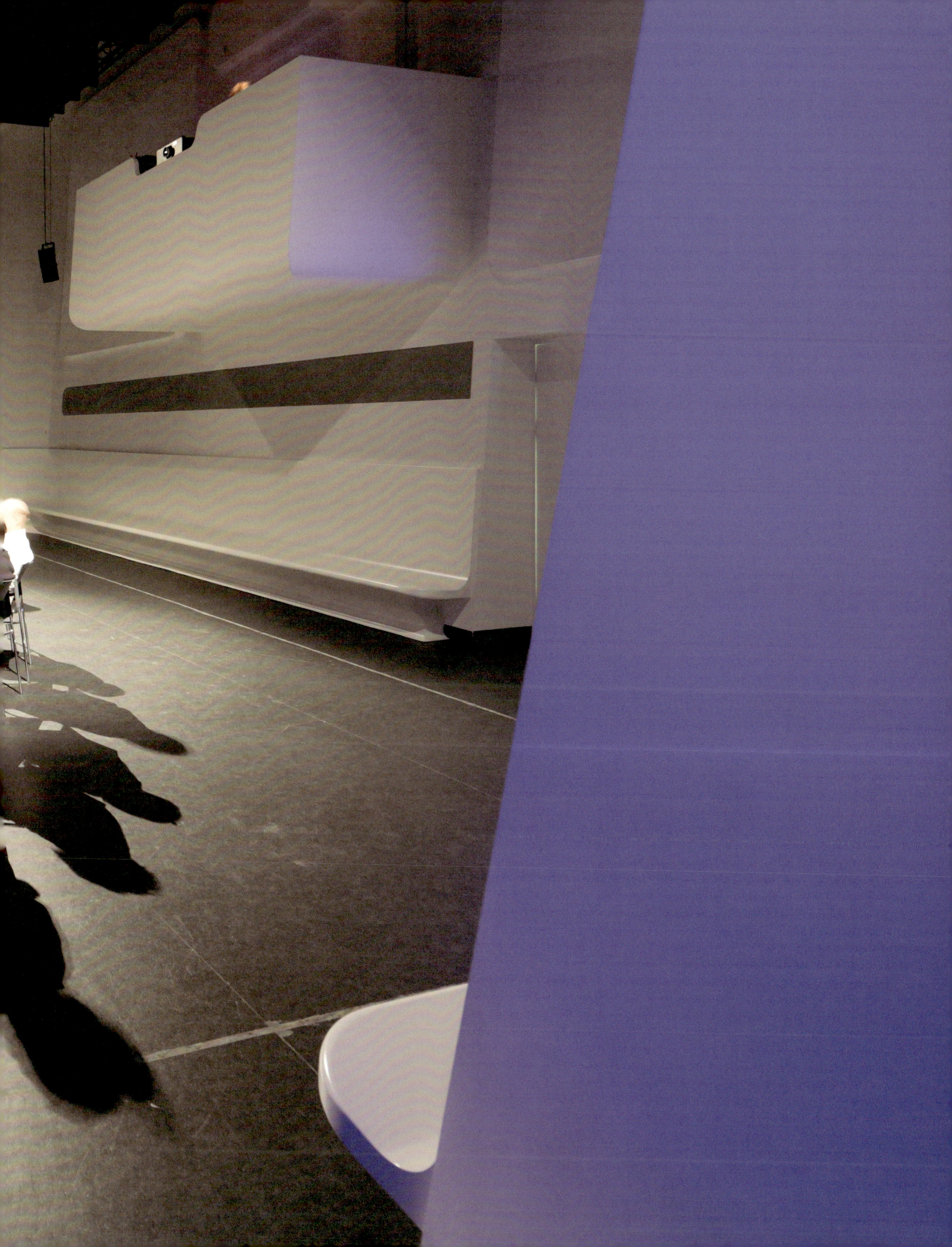

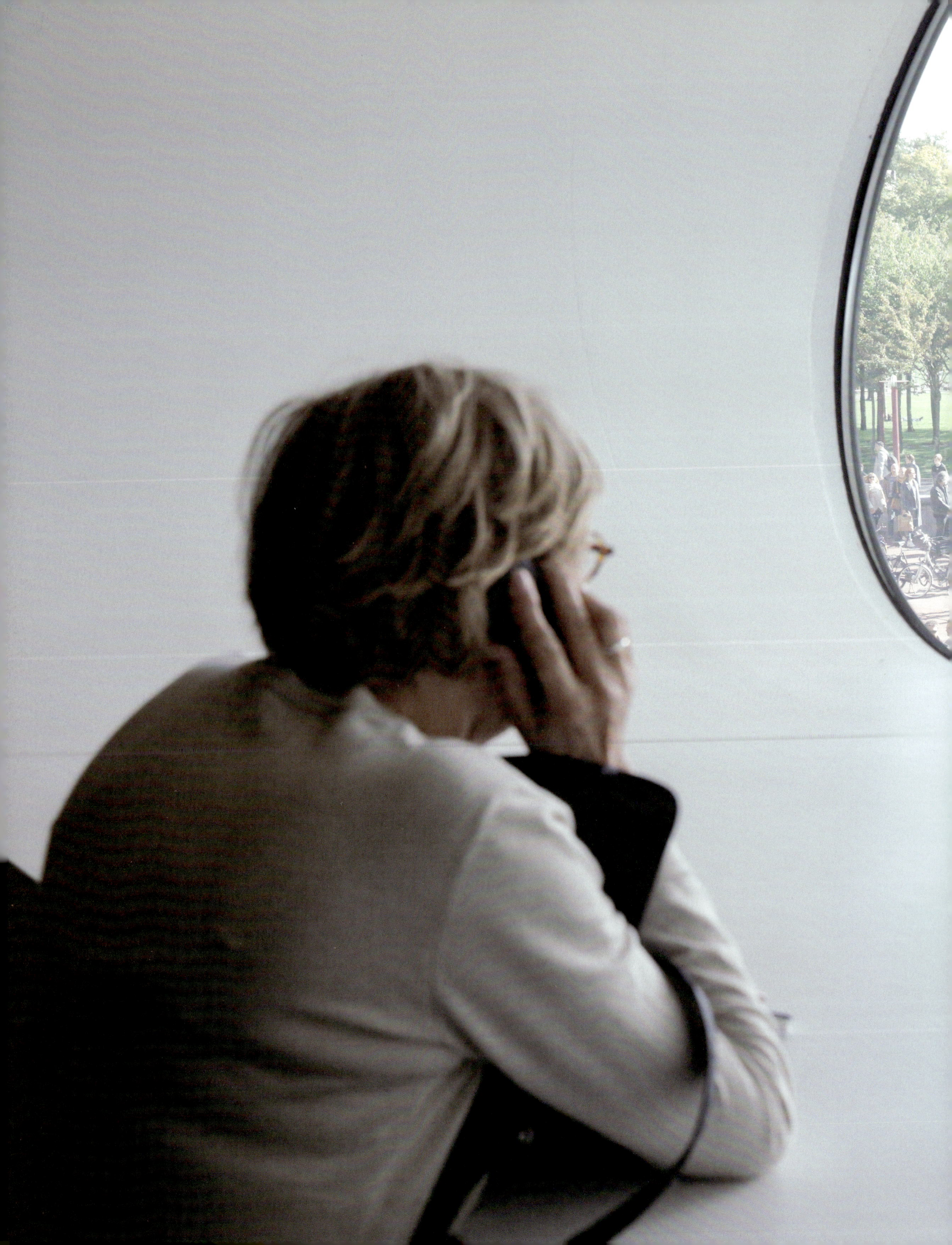

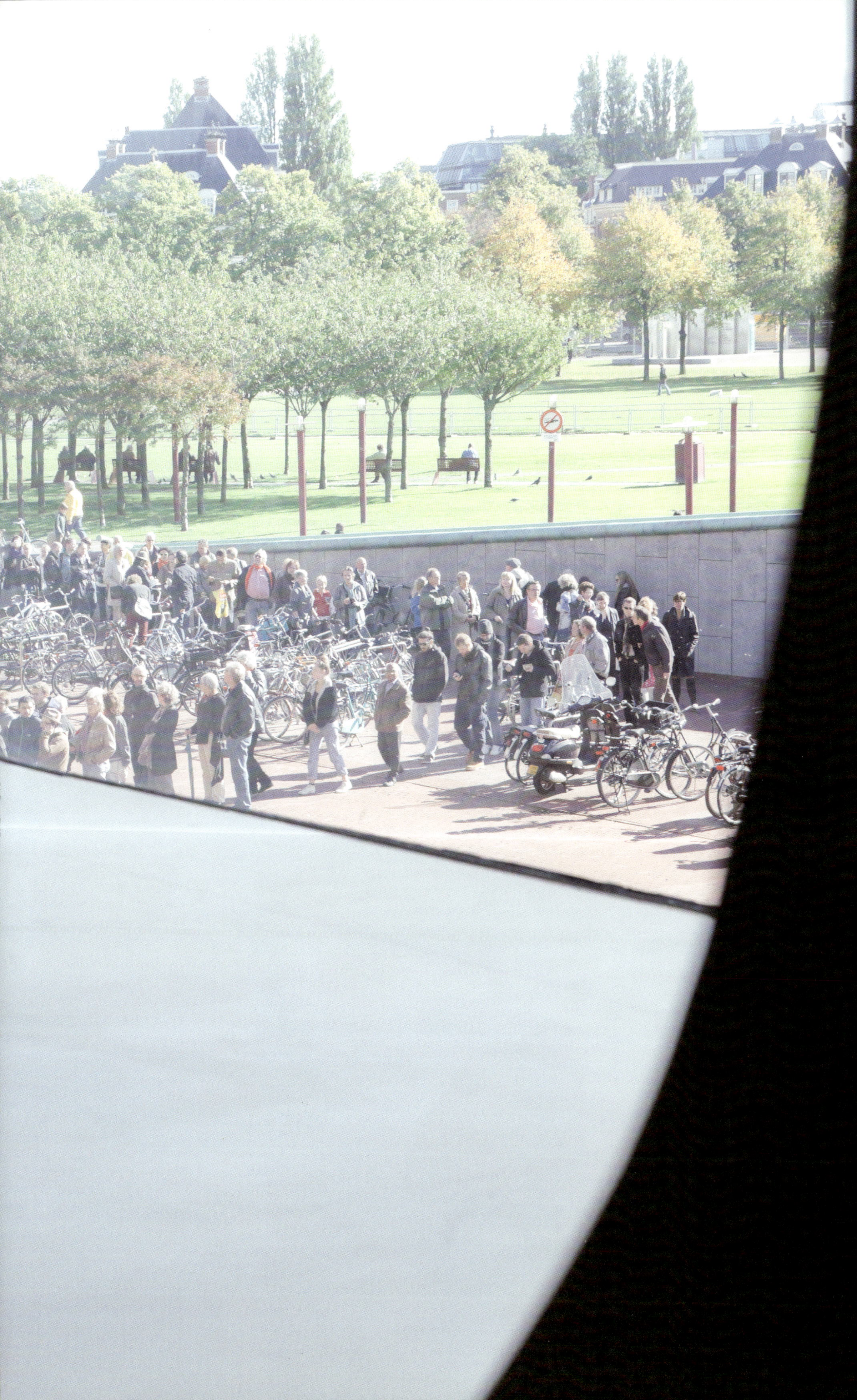

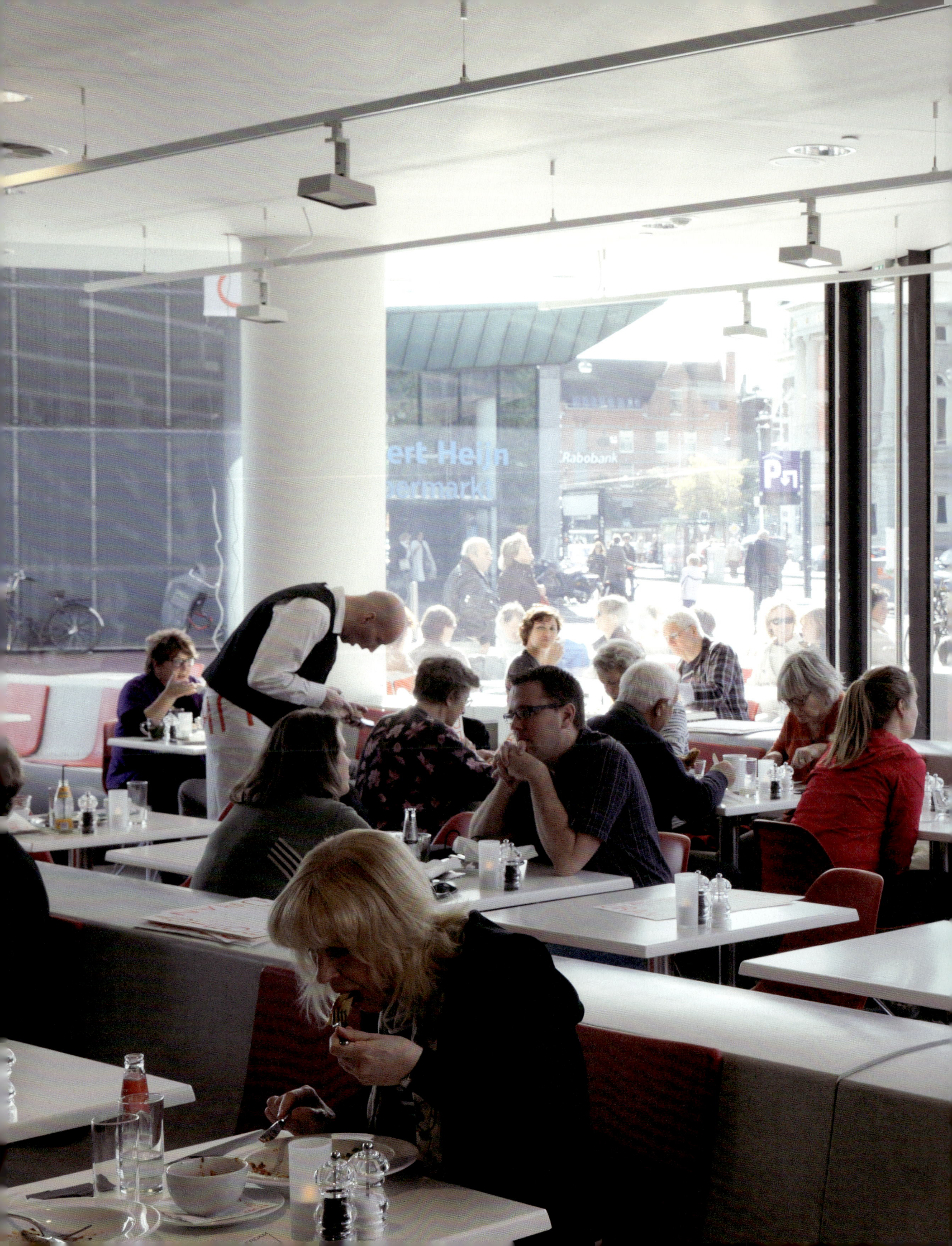
Rabobank

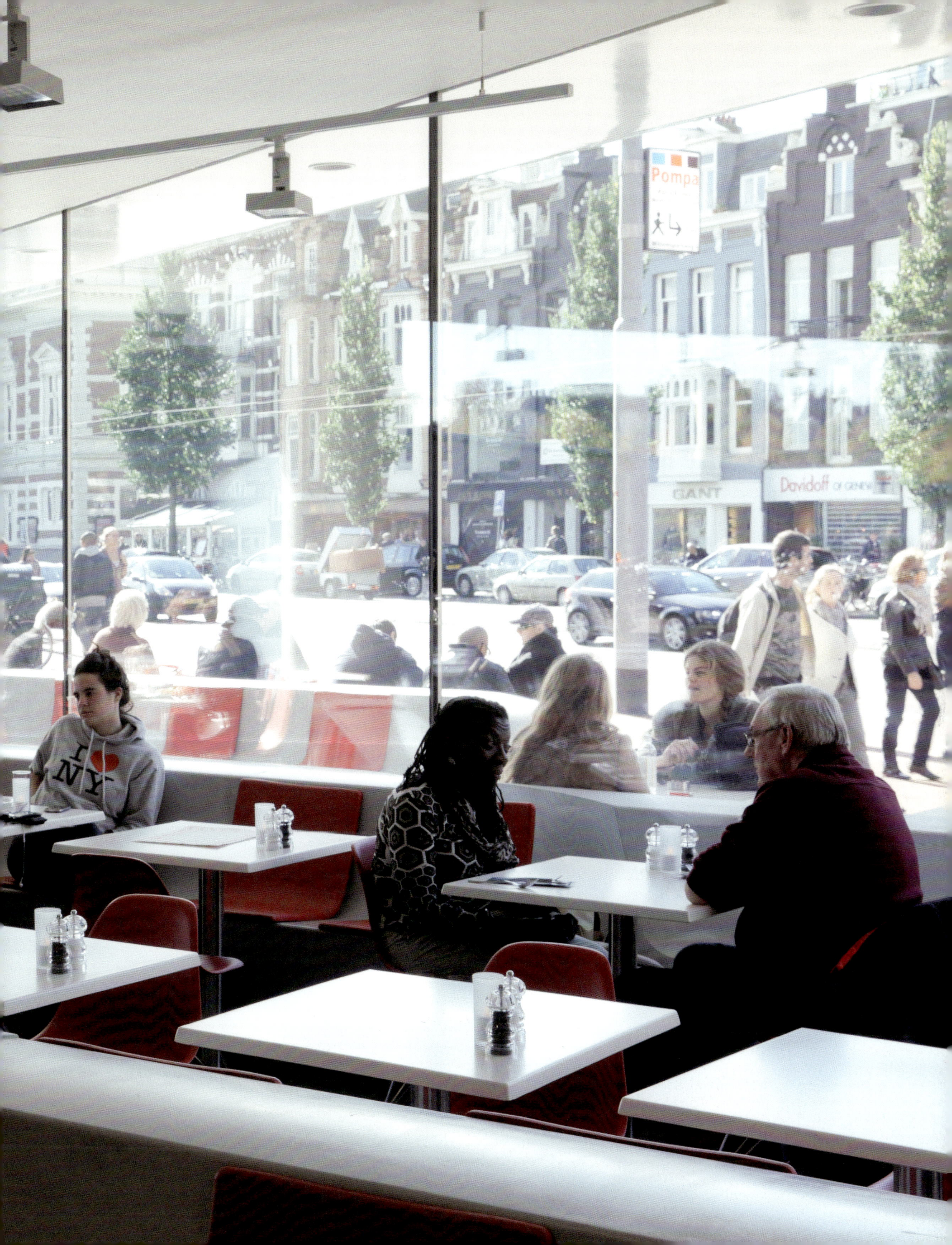
Pompa
GANT
Davidoff
I NY

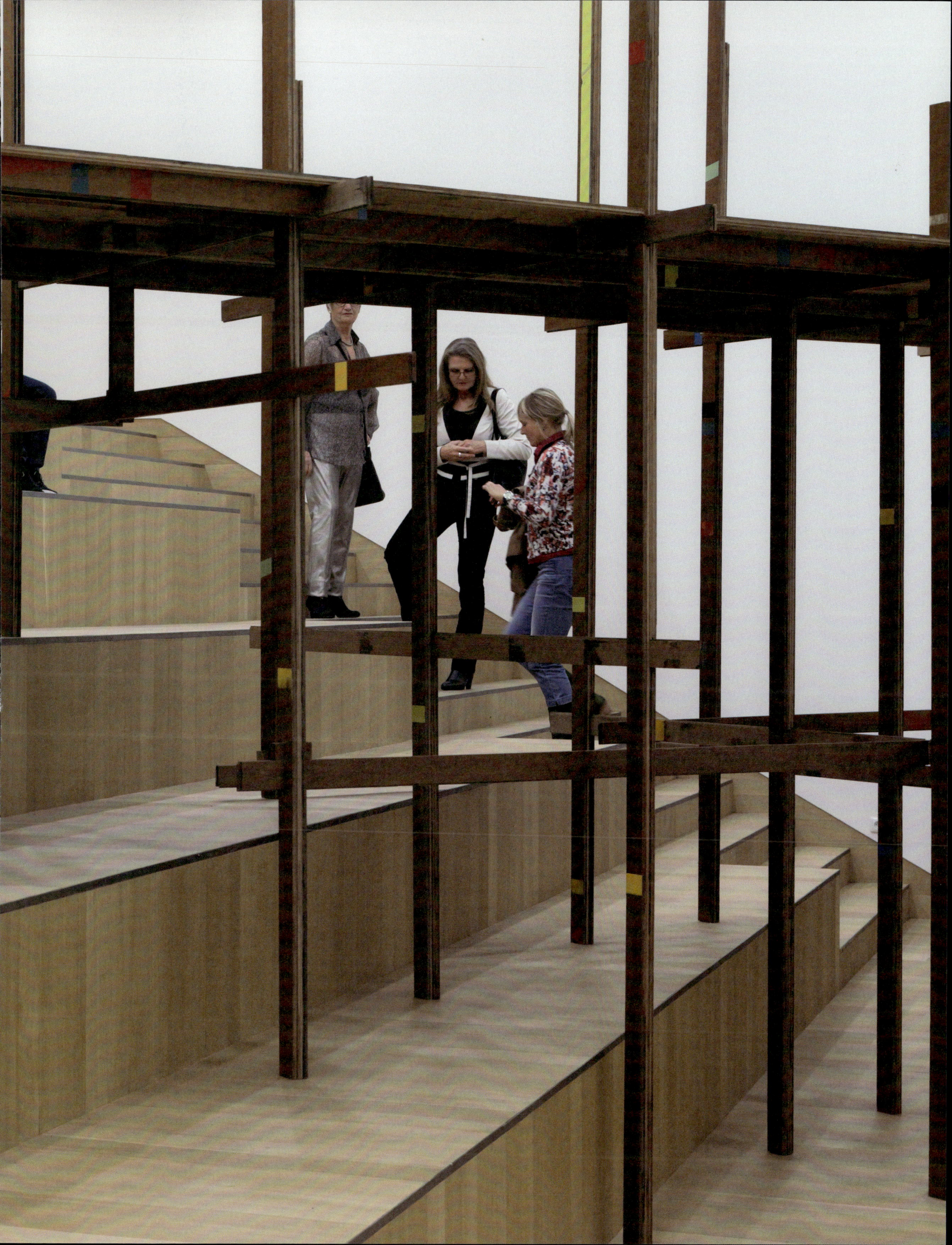

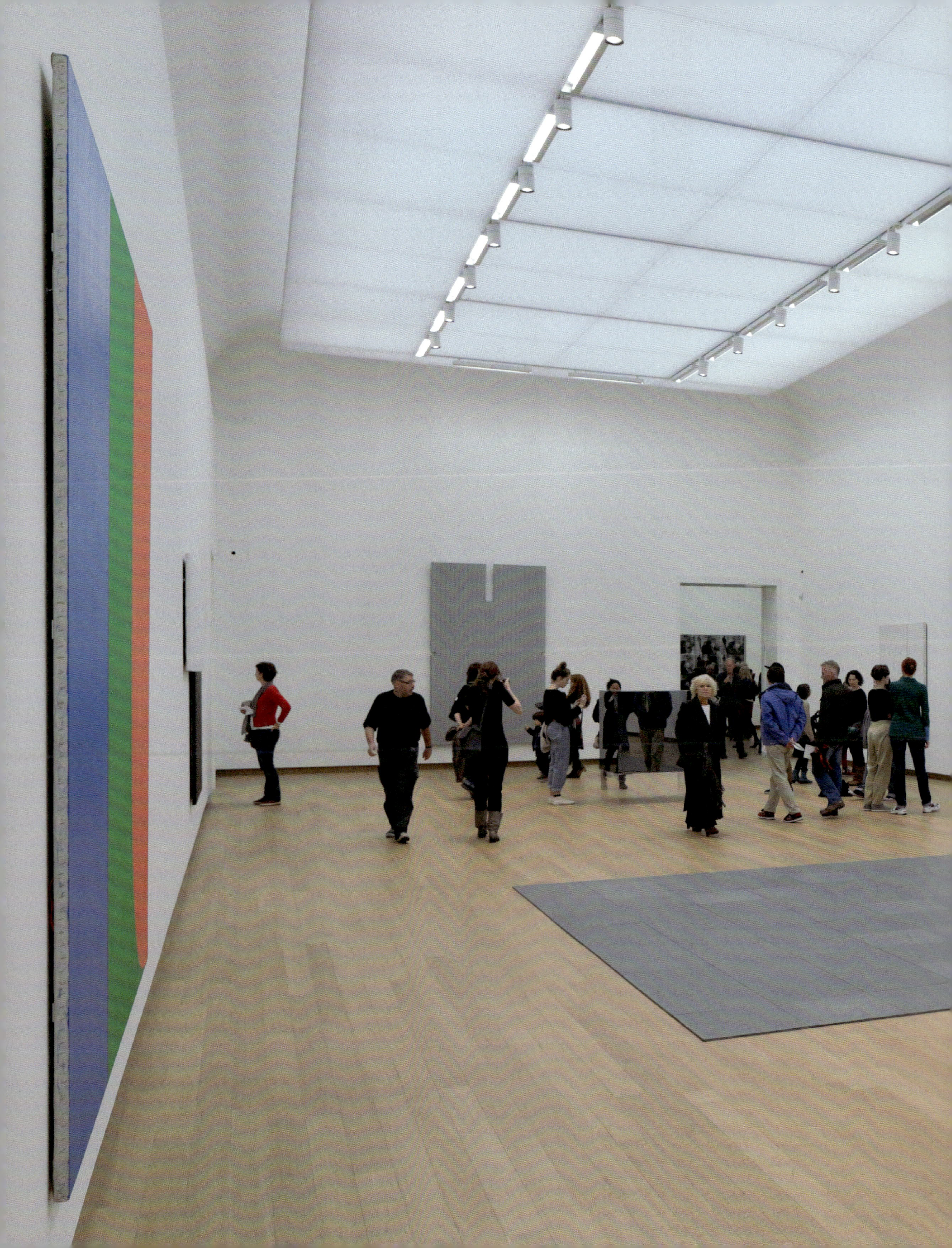

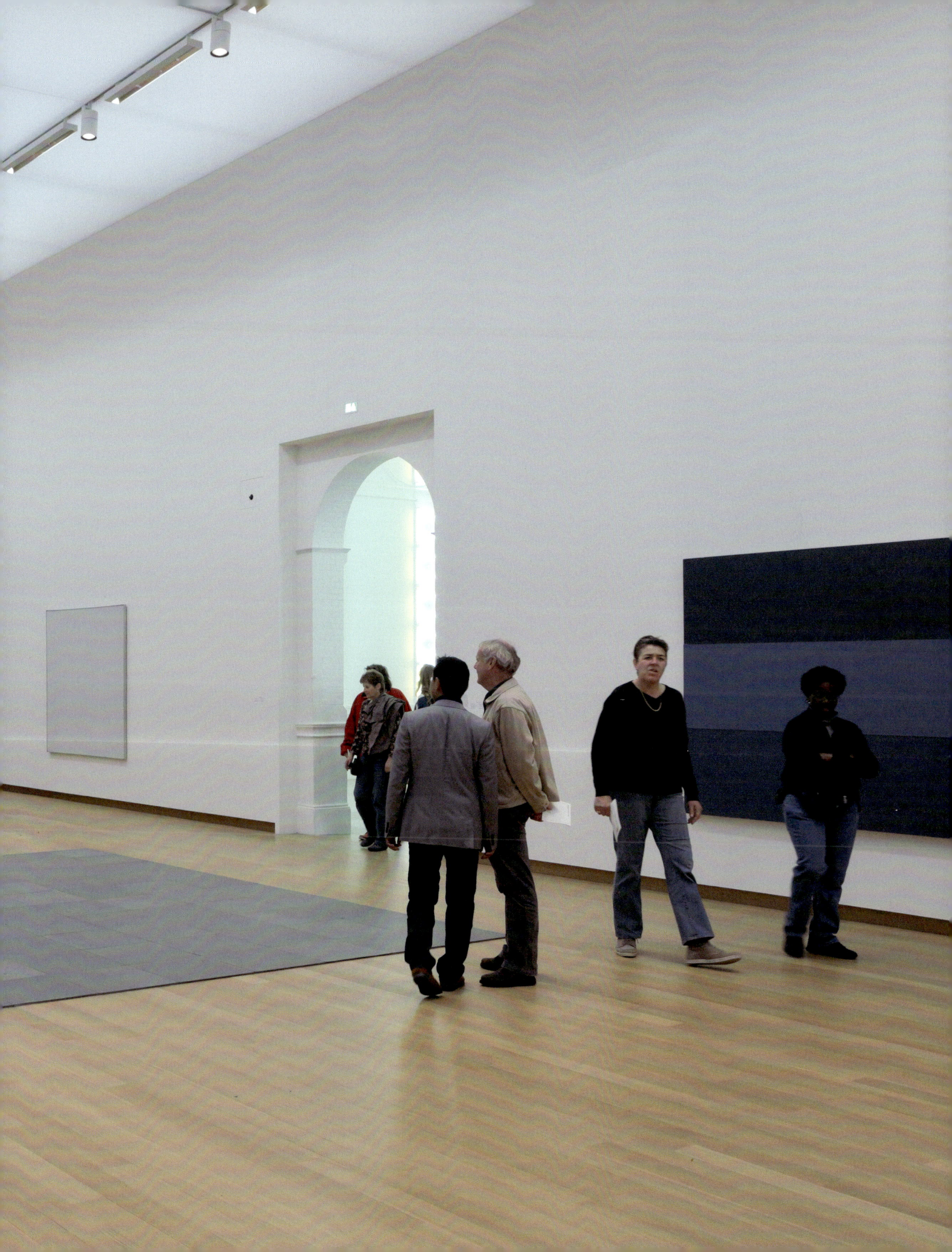

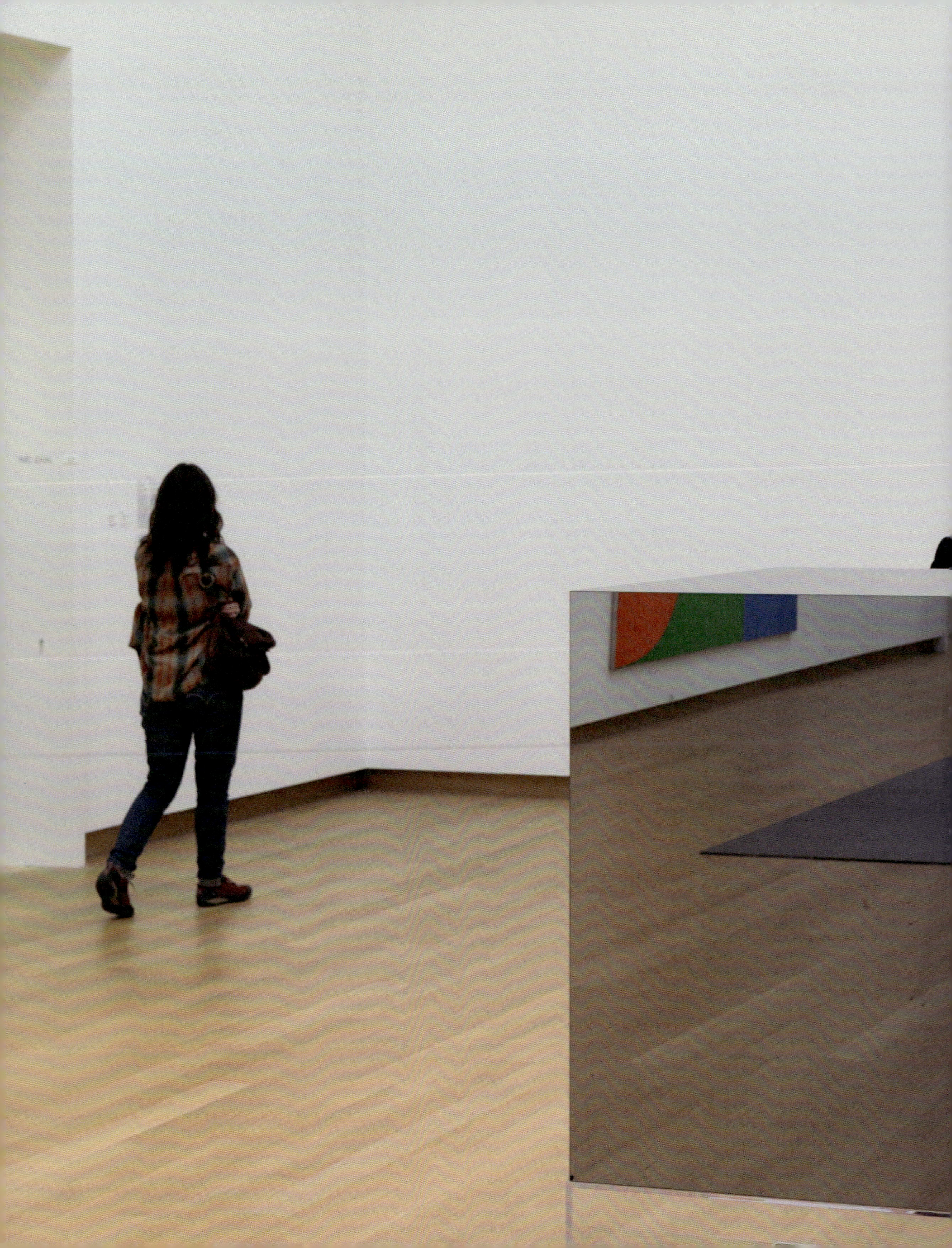

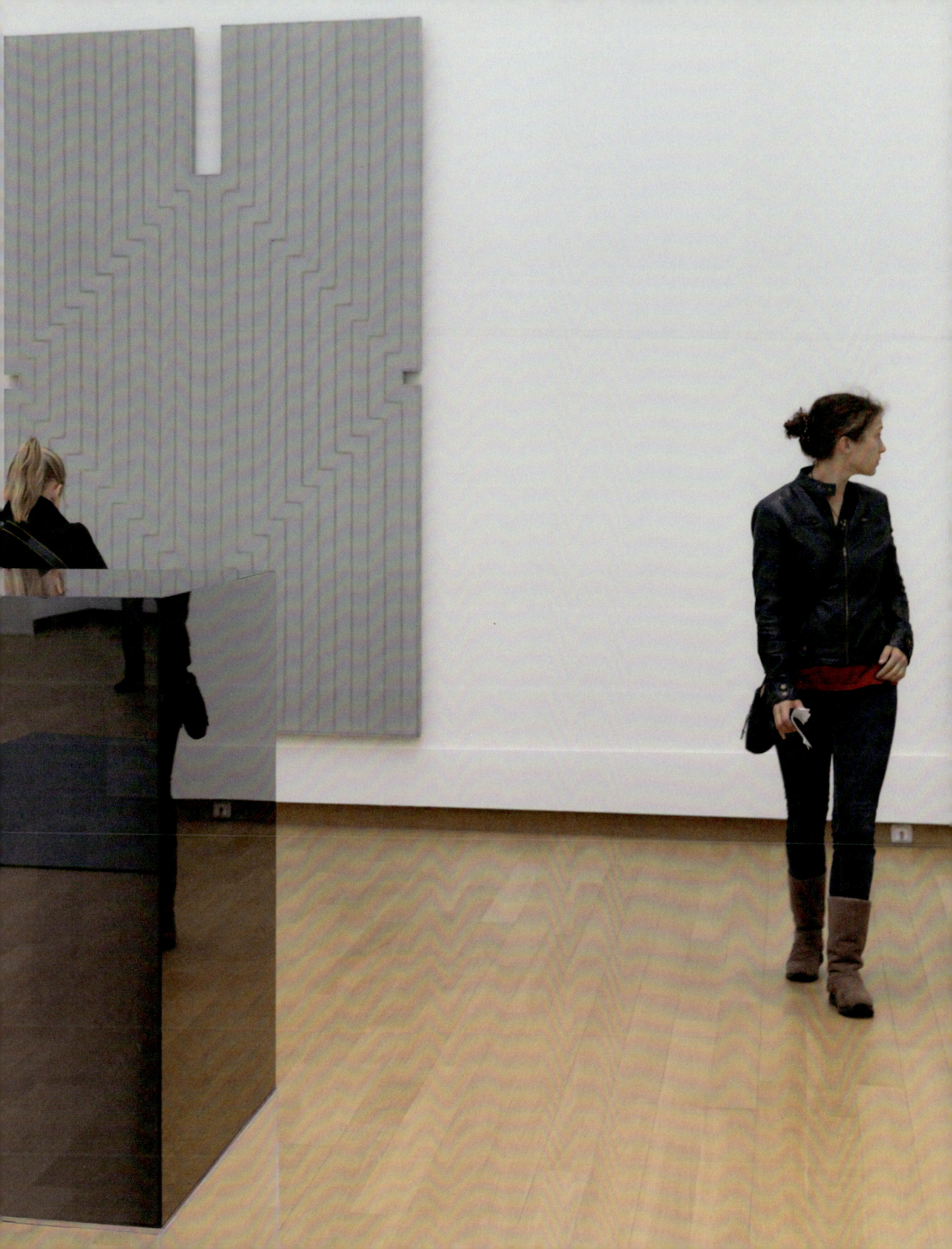

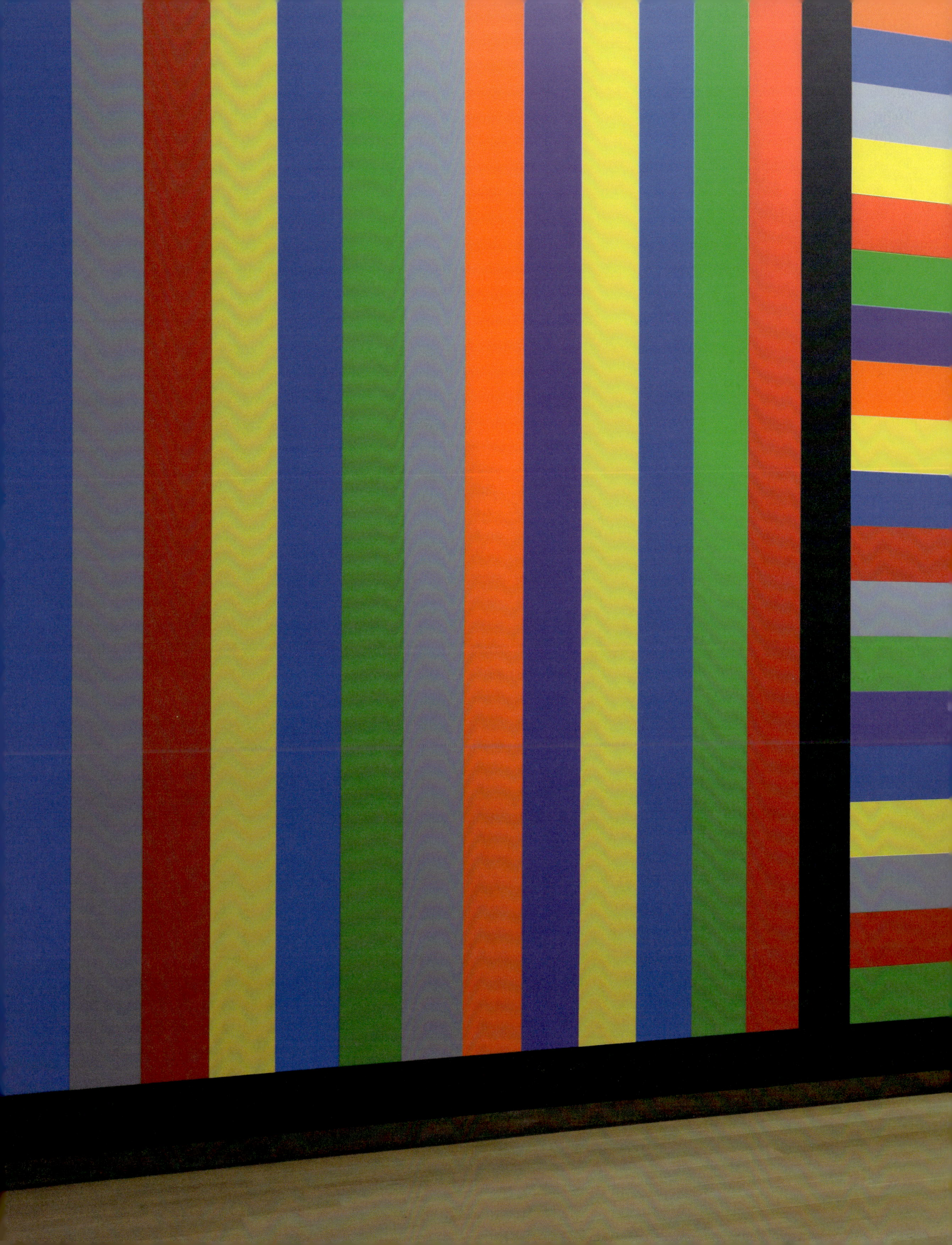

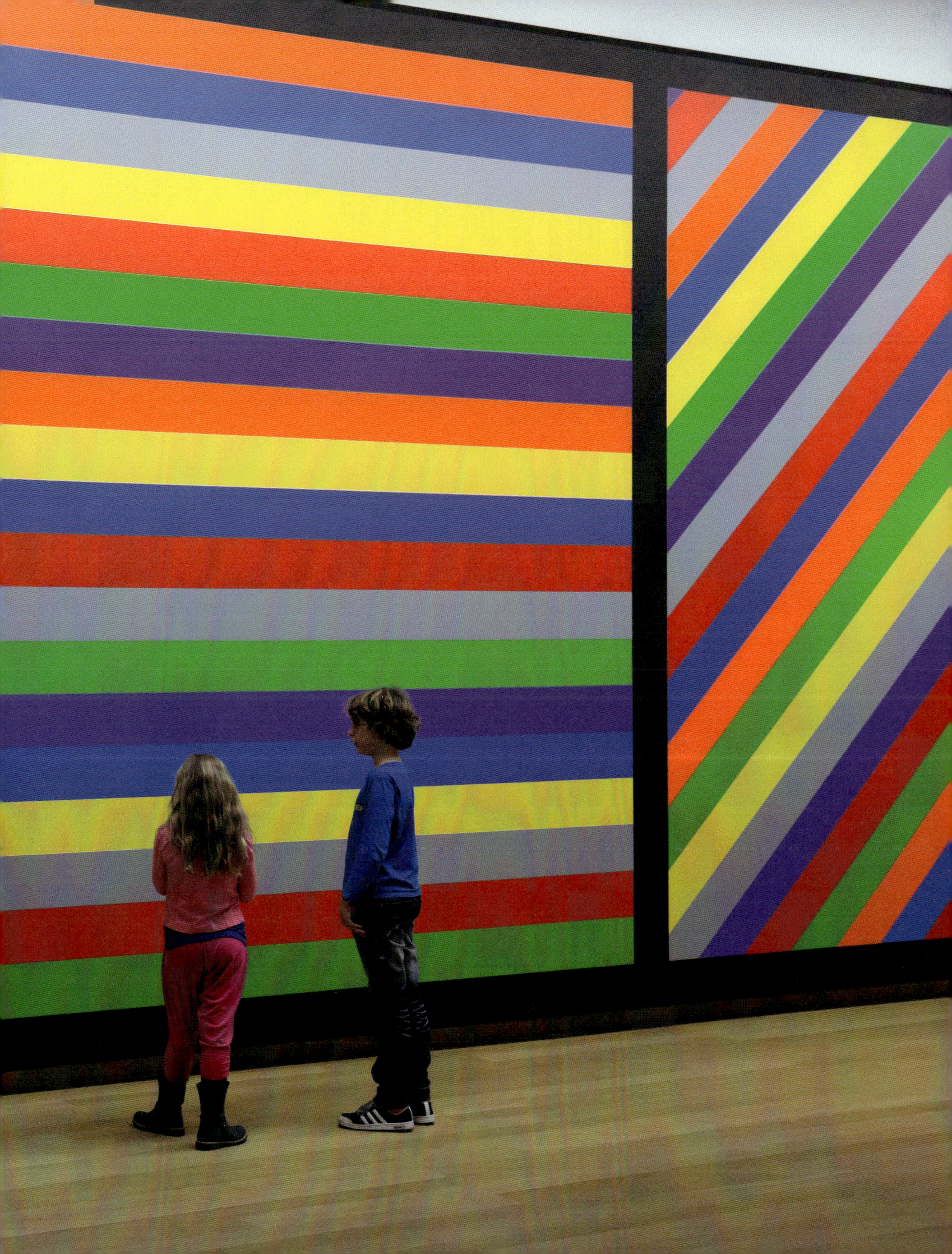

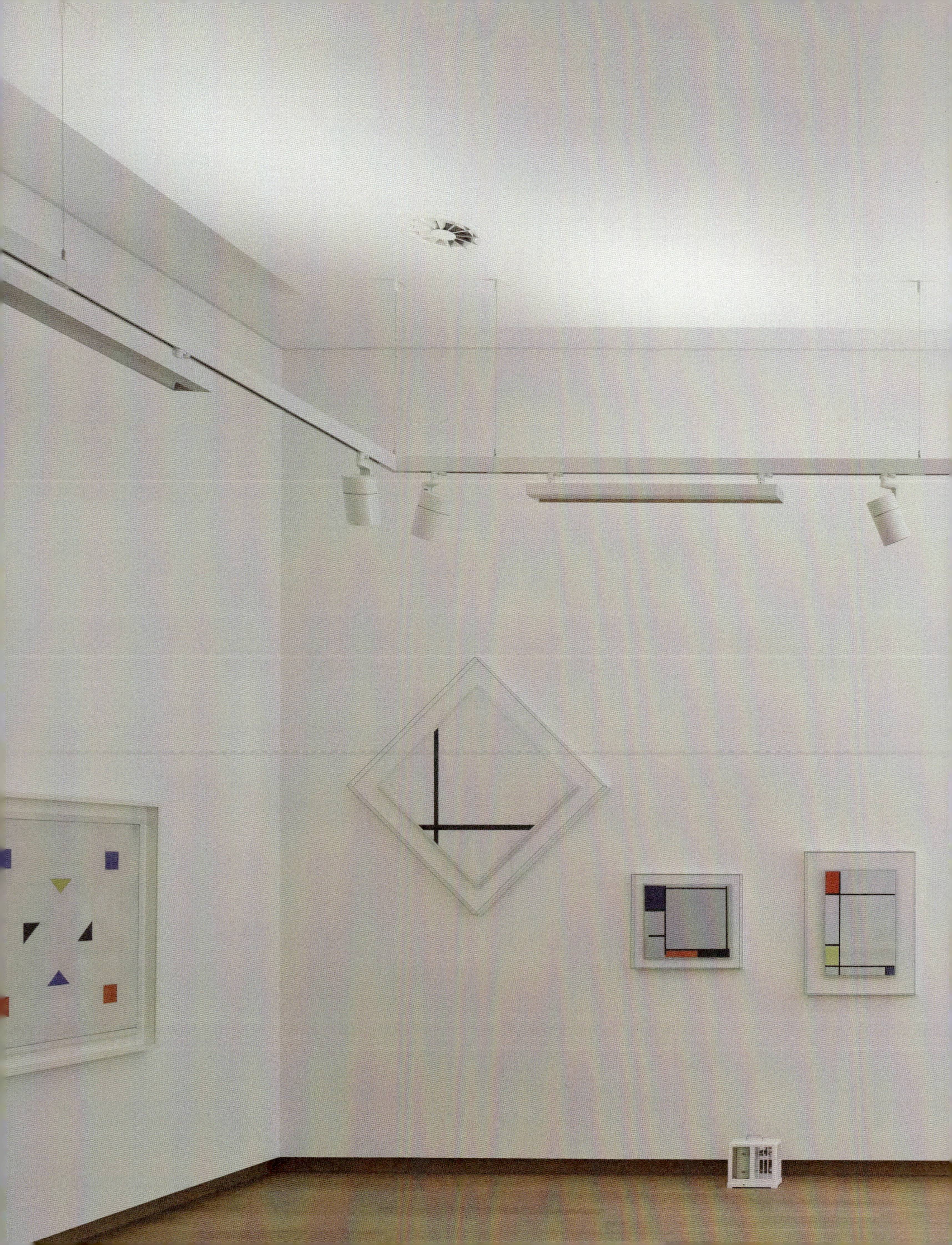

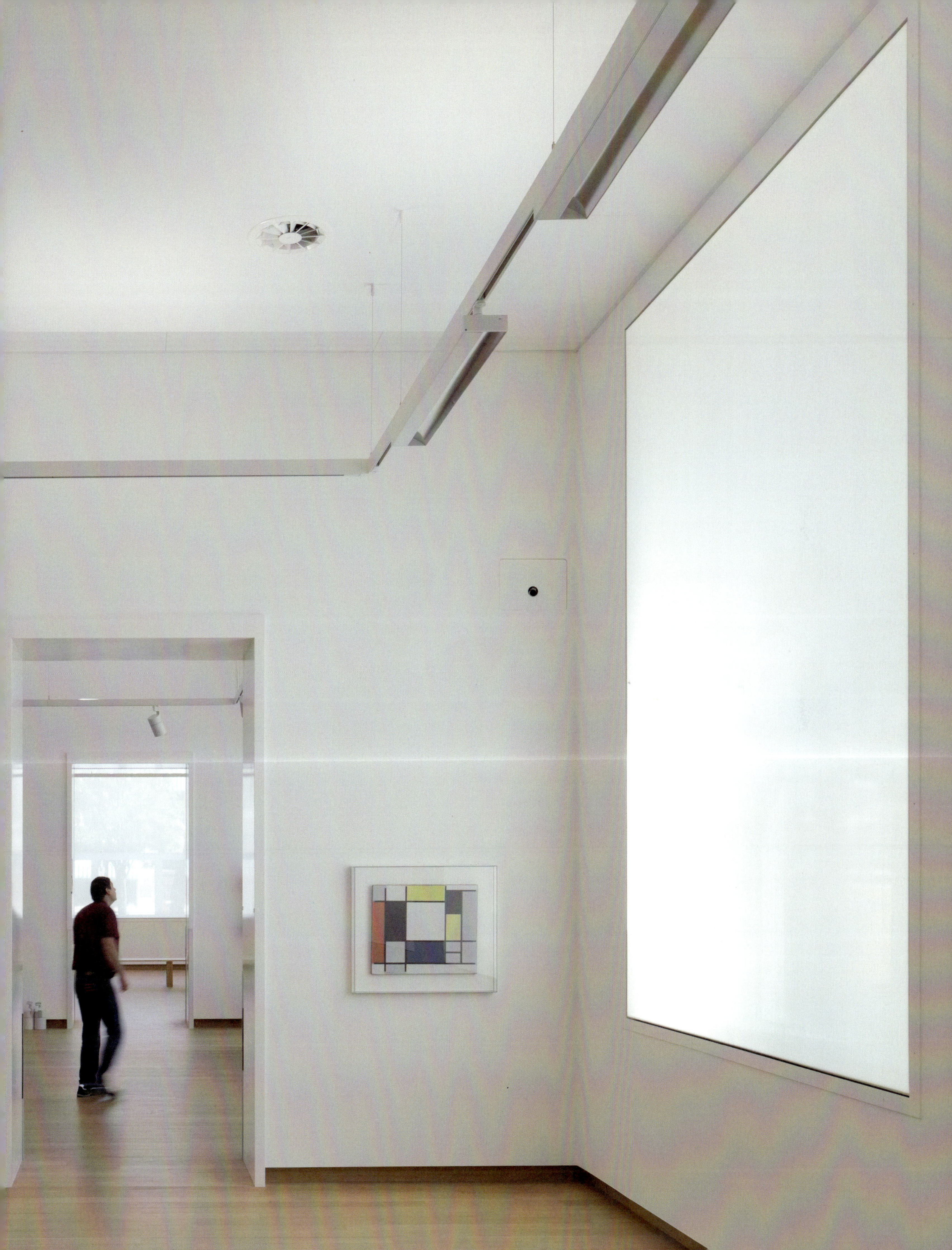

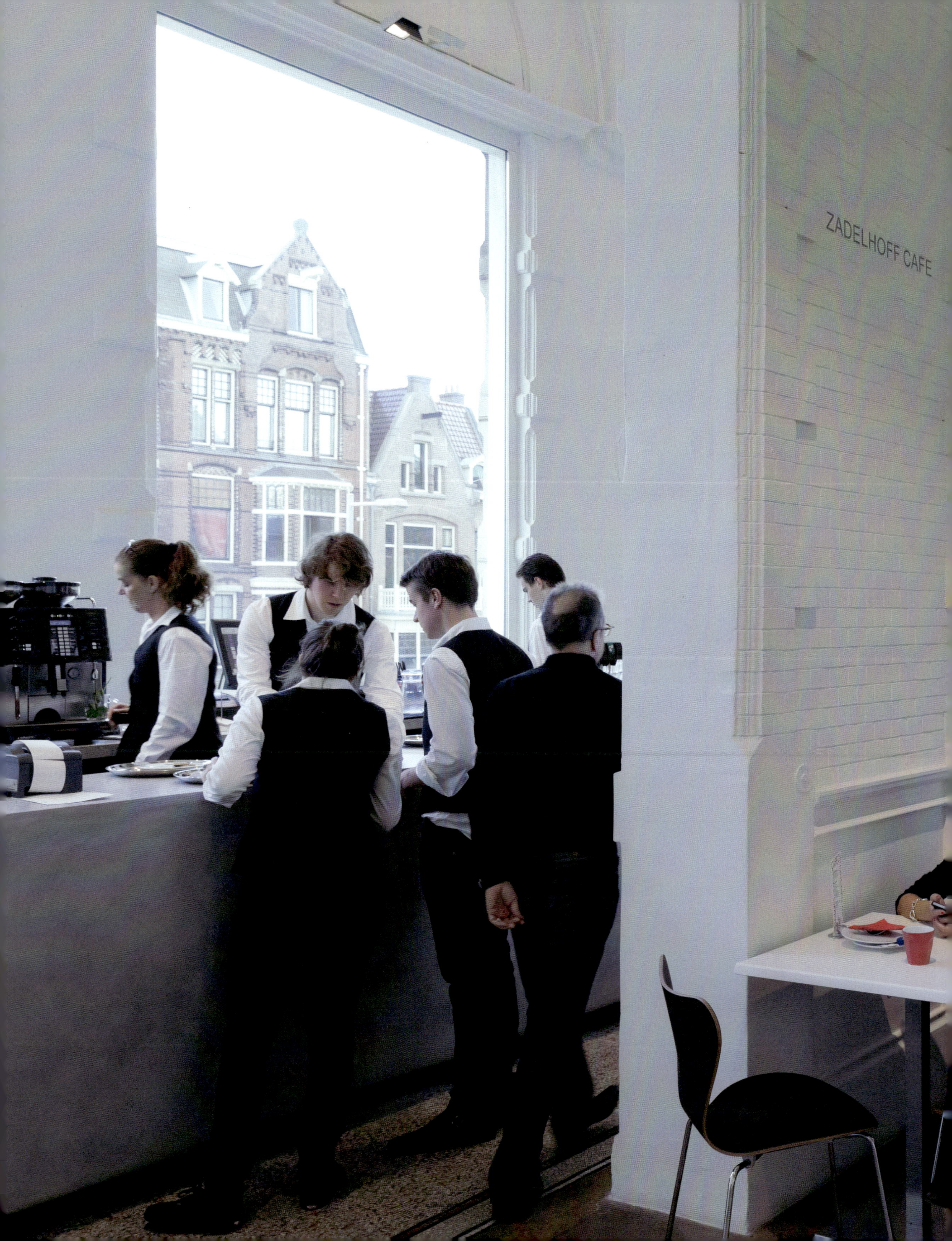
ZADELHOFF CAFE

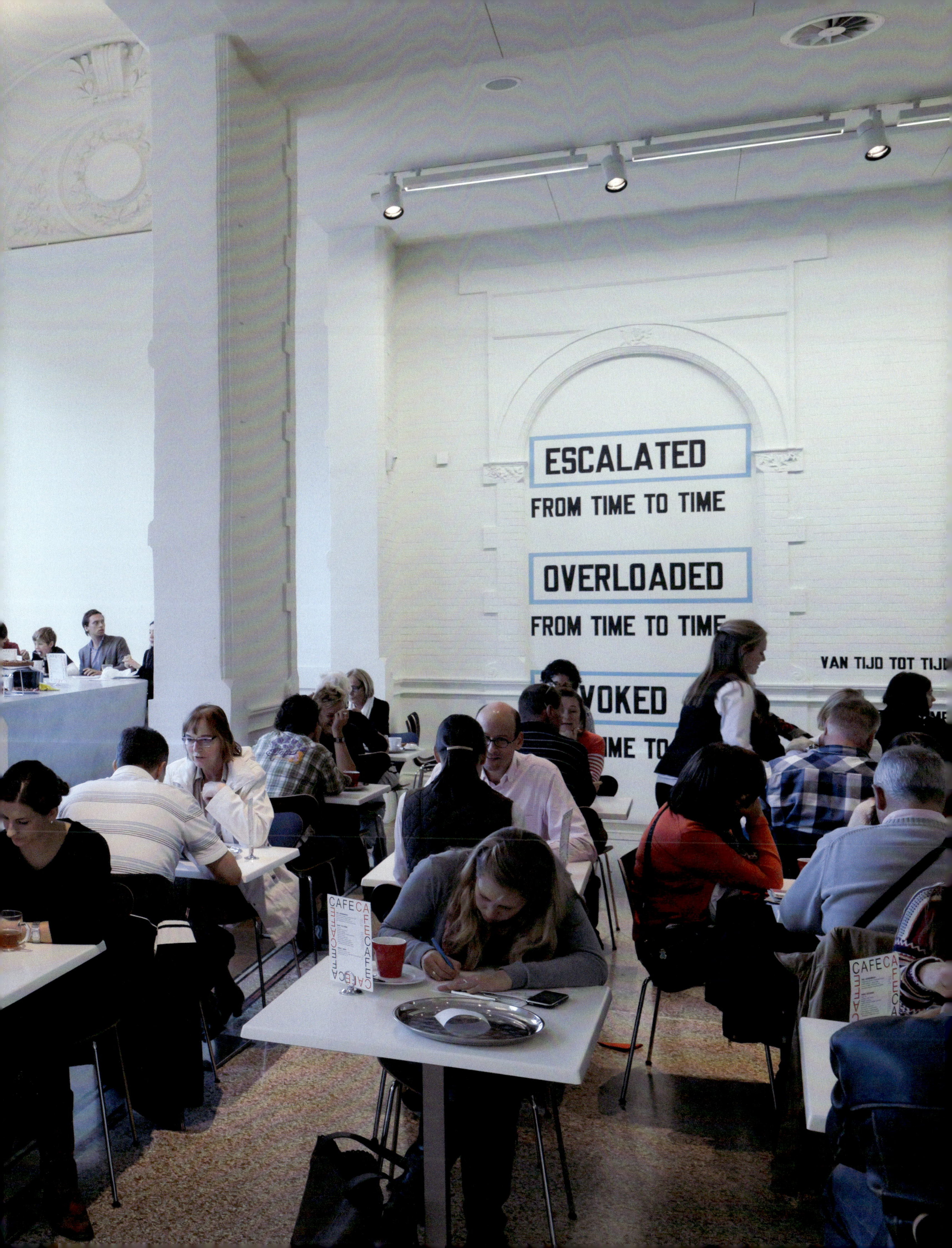
ESCALATED
FROM TIME TO TIME
OVERLOADED
FROM TIME TO TIME
VAN TIJD TOT TIJD

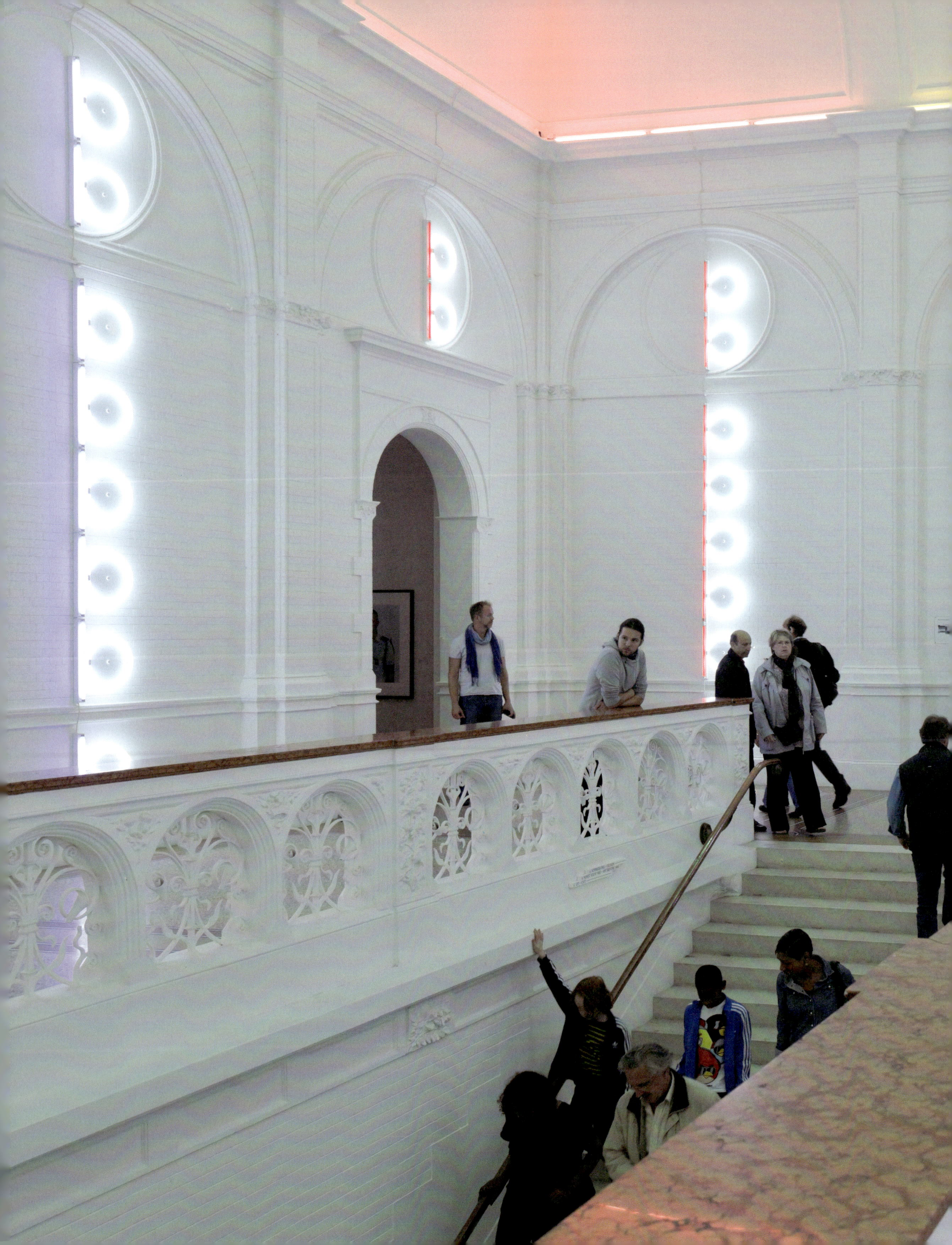

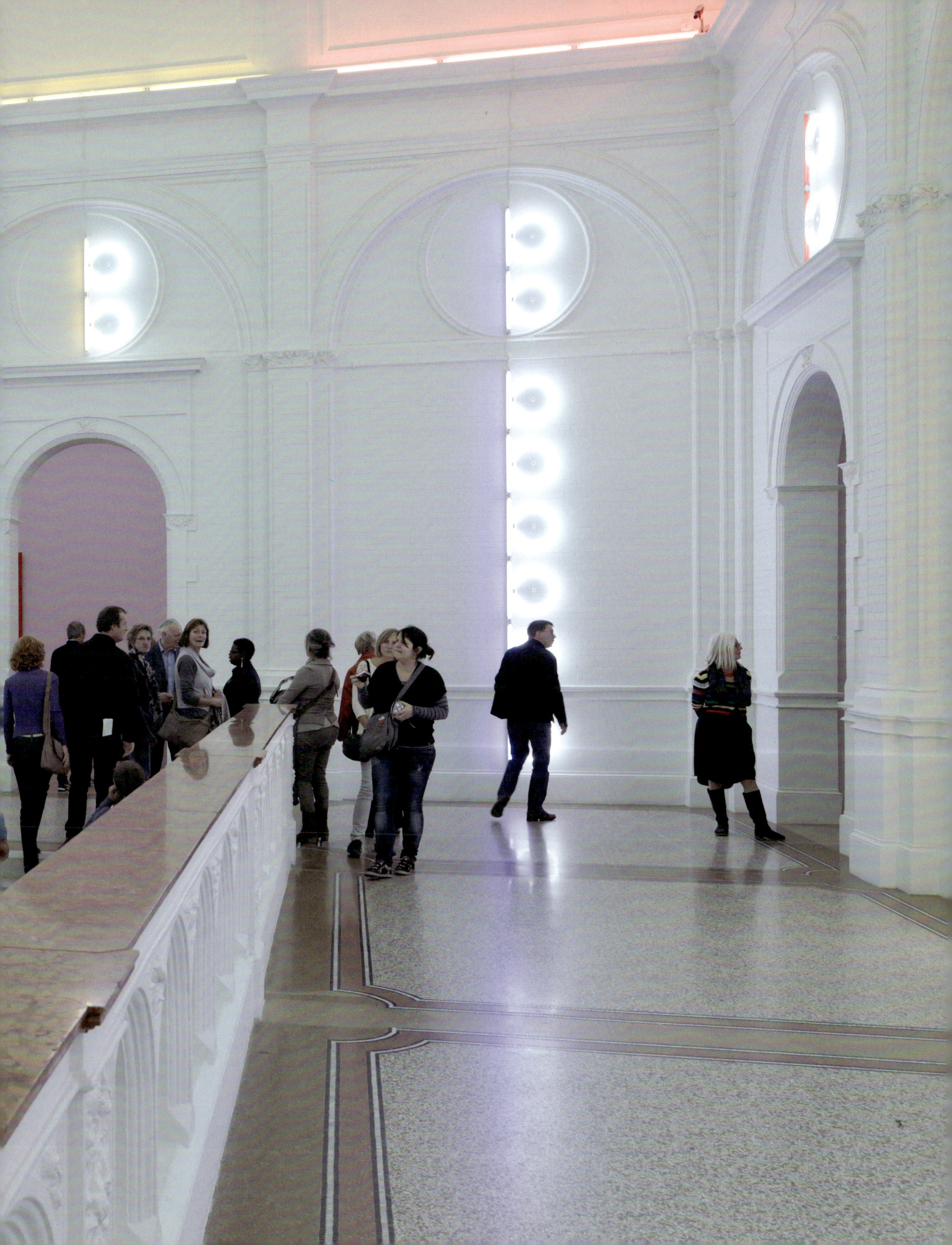

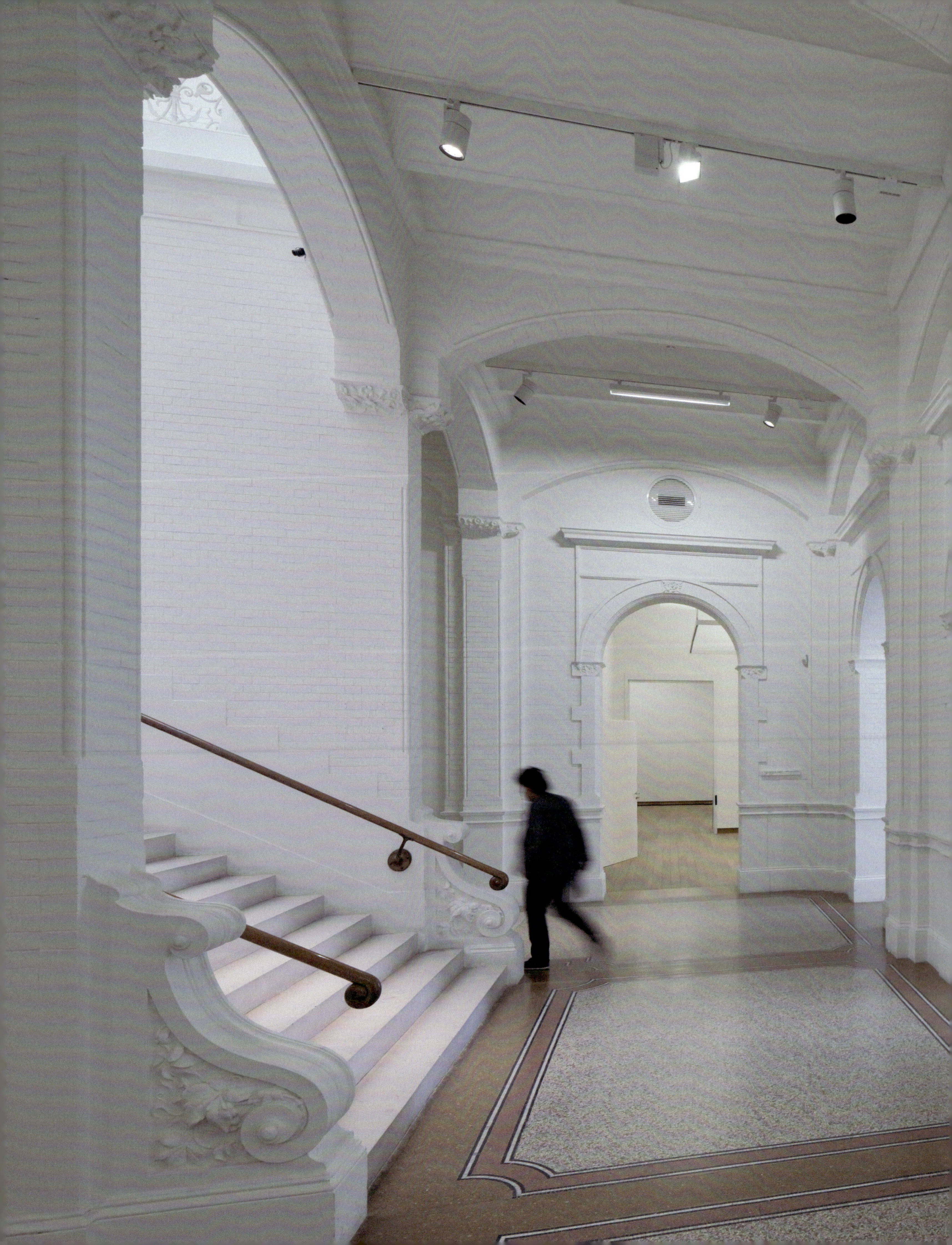

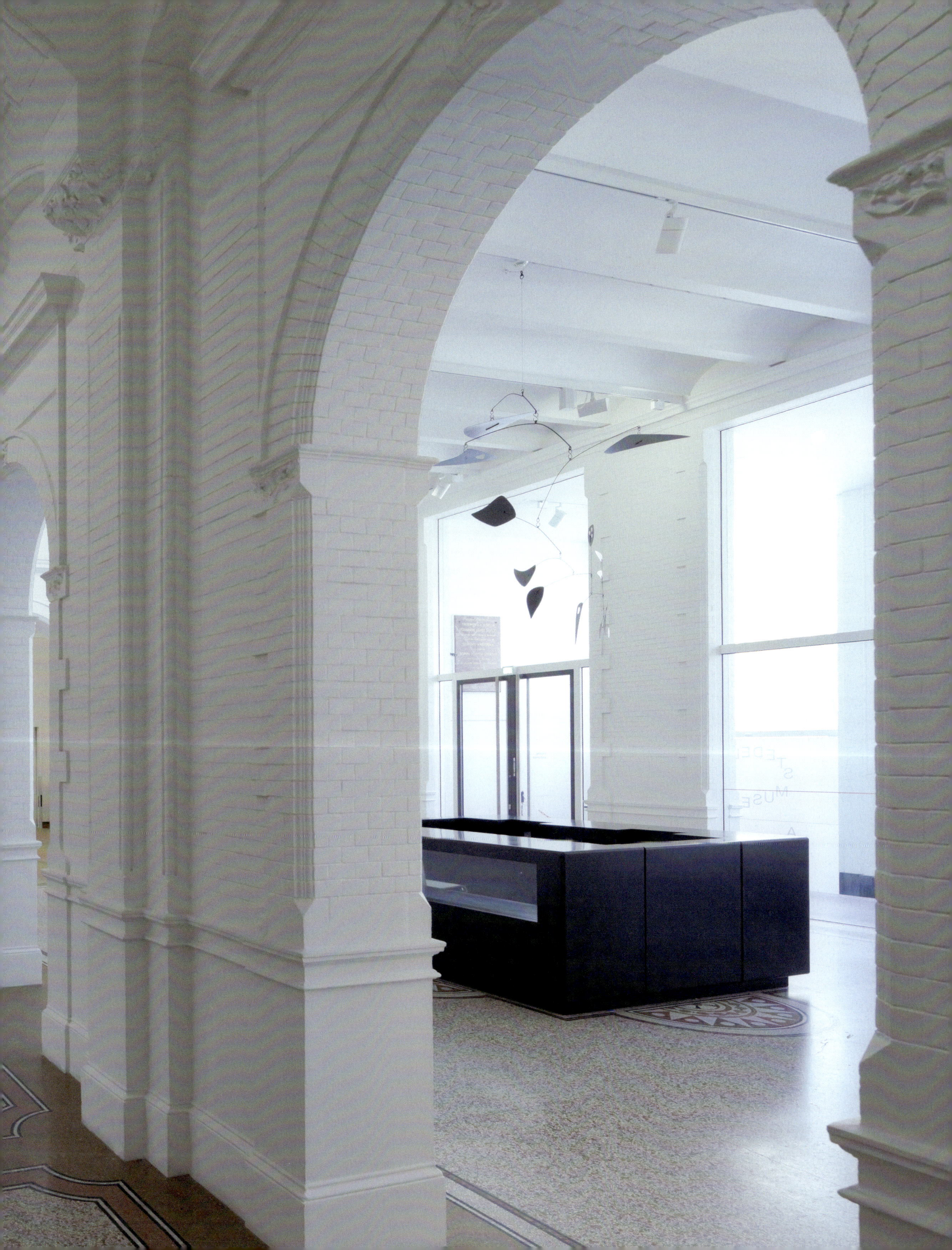

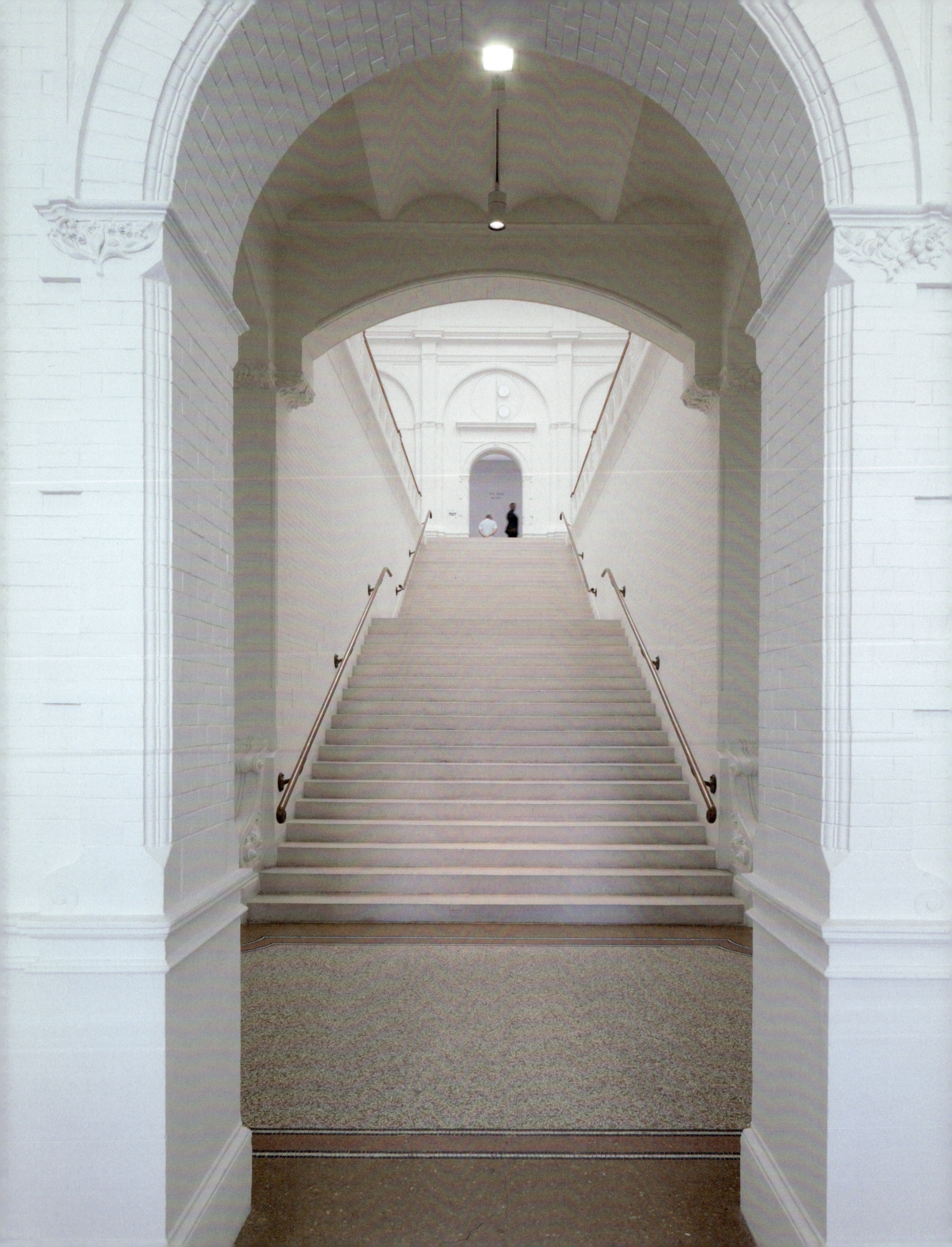

THE STEDELIJK MUSEUM SINCE 1895

The recent transformation of the Stedelijk Museum Amsterdam by Benthem Crouwel Architects is only the latest in a long history of alterations and renovations to a building that first opened its doors in September 1895.

The most eye-catching aspect of the new Stedelijk is the elegantly smooth, white bathtub-like extension with its great canopy, which seems to float above the entrance hall on the Museumplein. This impressive structure is made of a composite of synthetic resin with two types of reinforcing material: para-aramid fiber and carbon fiber. The resin component will expand as the temperature rises, but because of the contraction of the fibers the thermal expansion of the whole structure will be negligible. Using this innovative approach, this enormous structure could be built without any expansion joints, which would normally be required for a building of this size. Below the white structure is the entrance hall, containing the reception desk and cloakroom, the restaurant and the museum shop, enclosed by a glazed façade. The floor of the entrance hall runs through to the exterior, creating a sense of seamlessness between the interior and the square outside. With two monumental artworks, a wall hanging by Petra Blaisse's bureau Inside Outside (*Damast*) and a photograph by Louise Lawler, the entrance hall functions as a central juncture for the arriving visitor. To the left is the restaurant, to the right the bookshop and, a few steps up and straight ahead is the former garden room, now the Audi Gallery, providing access to the older building and the first exhibition spaces.

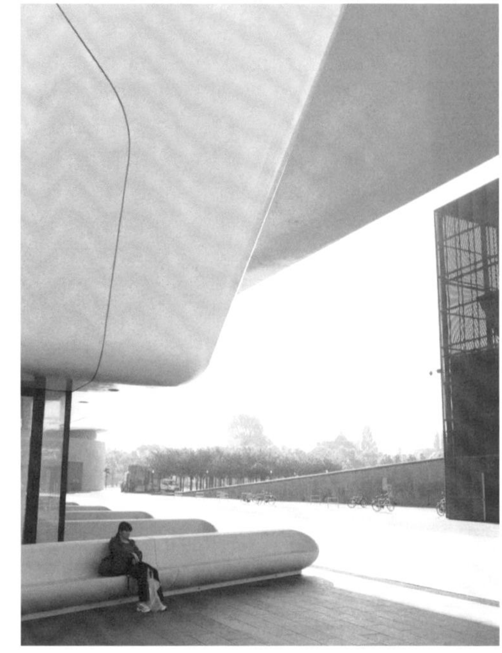

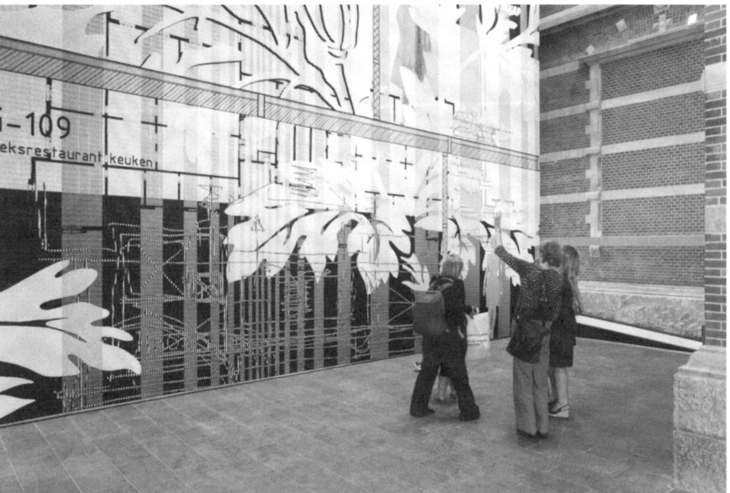

Damast, a wall hanging designed by bureau Inside Outside (Petra Blaisse and Marieke van den Heuvel) to a commission by the Stedelijk Museum Amsterdam, 2012. Produced by Desso.

The visitor now has a choice of routes, ascending staircases via the Hall of Honor on the first floor of the old building to emerge from either of a pair of walkways into the exhibition space in the new building, floating above the entrance hall. The first floor of the new wing also contains the new auditorium. From here an escalator provides access to the basement, where the exhibition route continues down to the subbasement. This colossal new two-storey exhibition space below the square is the pièce de résistance of the new wing. The library's reading room and educational studios are located in the upper basement, connecting to the entrance hall via a staircase. The basement also houses various museum facilities that aren't open to the public. A service entrance on the Van Baerlestraat also contains a service elevator, for transport of larger works of art; it provides access to the offices on the upper floors of the new wing. Apart from the service entrance on the Van Baerlestraat there is no sign of the intense activity required to keep the museum up and running. Upstairs, under a roof that echoes the historic building, is a light and airy office space, which houses a staff cafeteria and flexible work spaces.

The Stedelijk Museum was not originally designed to house modern and contemporary fine art, as it does today. It initially contained a highly diverse collection ranging from paintings to fully-furnished period rooms from historic buildings along Amsterdam's canals, as well as exhibition items from the Museum of Medicine and Pharmacology and a collection of weapons from the Amsterdam Civic Militias. Exhibitions at the Stedelijk Museum were equally diverse: alongside the arts and crafts on display there were also exhibitions devoted to efficiency and to historical topics such as Napoleon and the Bonaparte family.

The Stedelijk Museum began to collect modern art in 1909, but the collection and the exhibitions continued to cover a wide spectrum for a considerable time, including a permanent installation about the history of Amsterdam, originally created in 1906. The Stedelijk took on its role as a museum specifically for modern and contemporary art, including applied arts and architecture, under the leadership of Willem Sandberg, who was director from 1945 to 1962. The remainder of the Stedelijk Museum collection found a home at the Amsterdam Historical Museum (now the Amsterdam Museum), which opened originally in De Waag in 1926, relocating in 1975 to the former city orphanage (Burgerweeshuis).

The historic Stedelijk Museum building, facing the Paulus Potterstraat and backing onto the Museumplein, was designed by Adriaan Willem Weissman (1858–1923), who was Amsterdam's city architect from 1891 to 1894. Weissman, two years younger than H. P. Berlage and six years older than W. Kromhout, was not the most innovative architect of his generation. The museum, designed in the style of the Dutch Renaissance, has a symmetrical layout

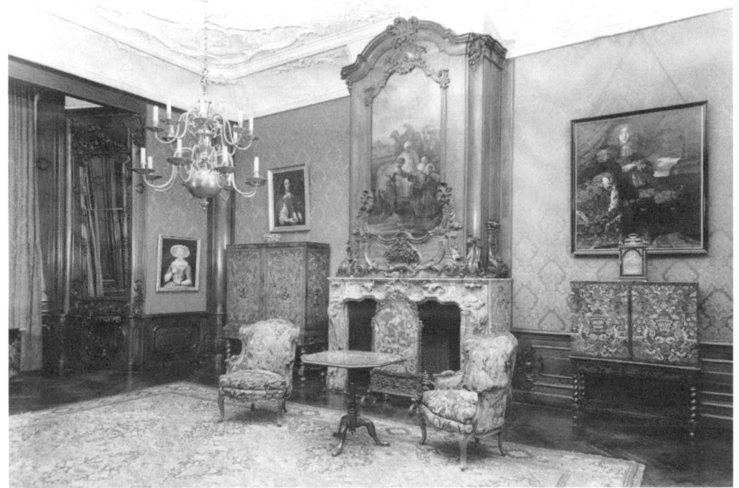

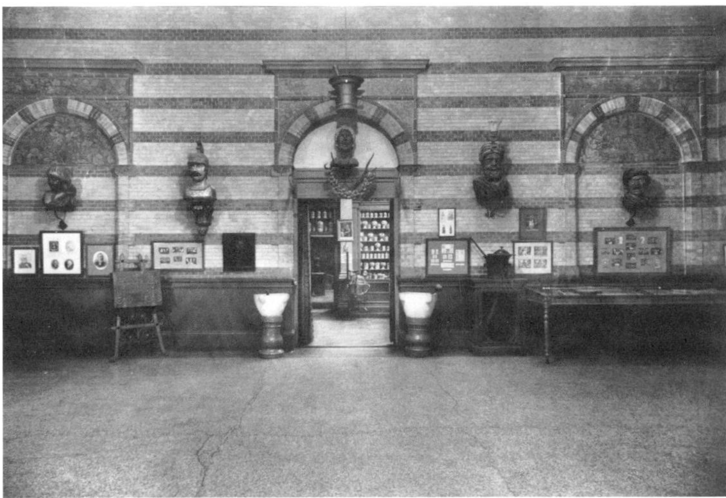

One of the period rooms (above) and the entrance to the Medical-Pharmaceutical Museum (below). 'The Stedelijk Museum was not originally designed to house modern art as it presently does. The museum initially contained a highly diverse collection ranging from paintings to fully furnished period rooms from fine buildings along Amsterdam's canals.'

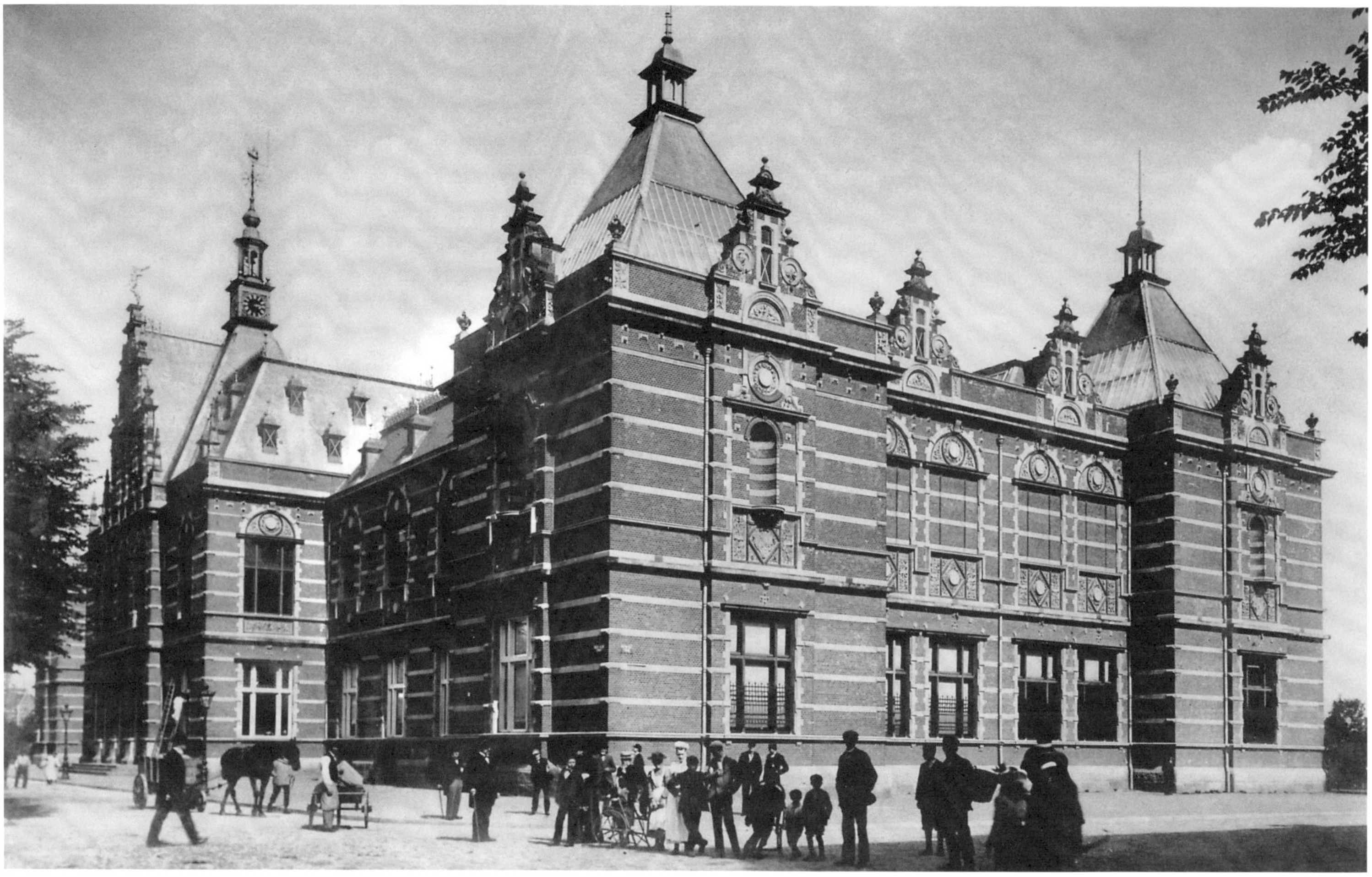

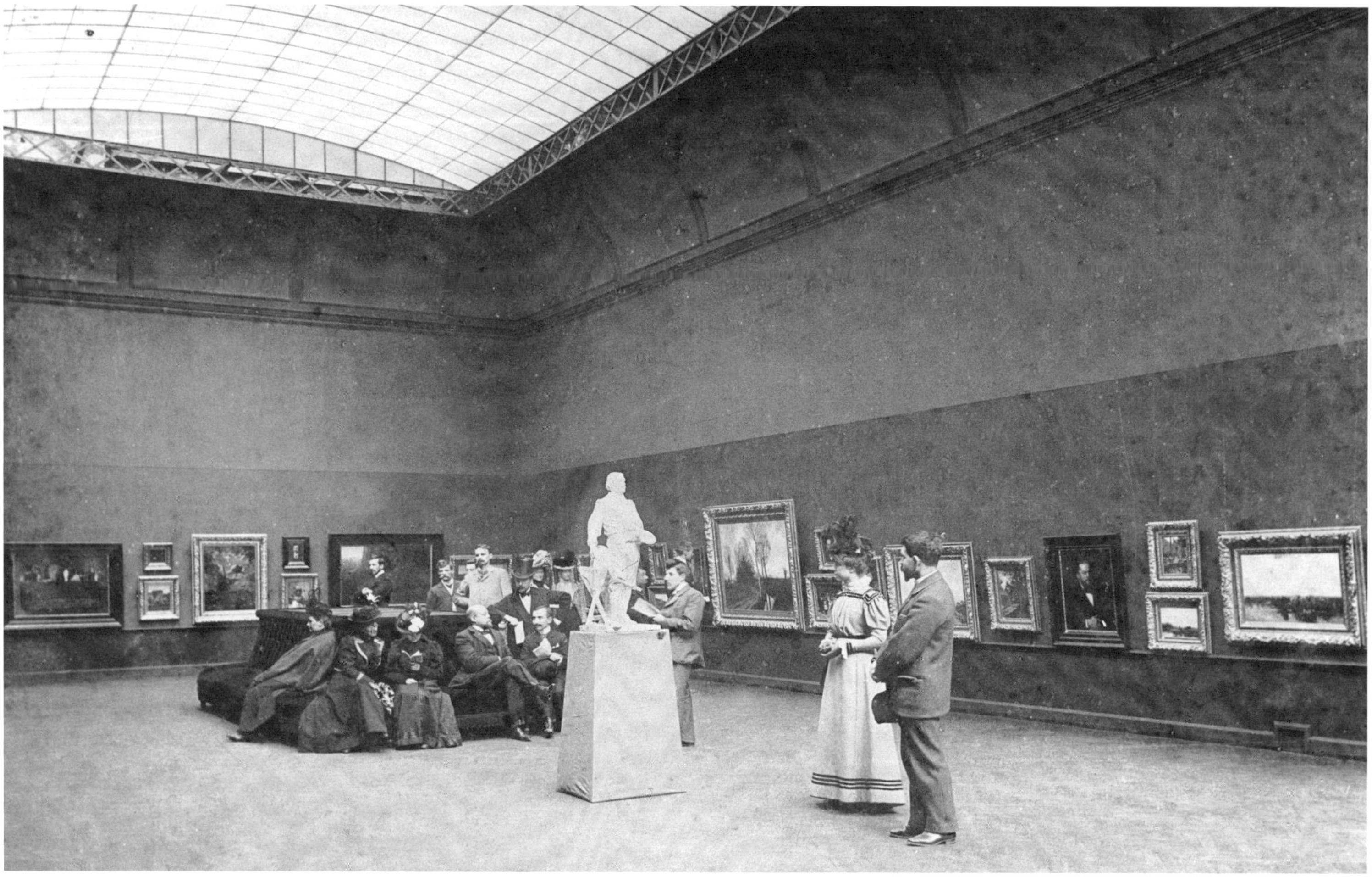

The exterior of the Stedelijk Museum and the Hall of Honor, shortly after the Museum's opening in 1895. Both inside and out, the building featured decorative elements referring back to a golden era of national history.

with a central entrance hall leading to a monumental staircase.

Both inside and out, the building featured decorative elements referring back to a golden era of national history. These are still visible on the exterior, but inside they have more or less disappeared in the course of successive alterations and renovations. The last remaining tile mural on the first floor vanished with the most recent transformation. Weissman's architecture for the museum came under heavy criticism from his professional colleagues when the building first opened. Kromhout, who later created the American Hotel on the Leidseplein, penned an article in *Architectura*, the journal of the Architectura et Amicitia architects' association, which he edited. His critique of the new museum was harsh:

> "And everyone who strongly believes as I do that architecture is the first among the arts, everyone who understands the value of a true monument will regret that a museum of such importance has been conceived with such a poverty of spirit."[1]

Four weeks later, the same journal carried a summary of the criticisms of the Stedelijk Museum that had appeared in other periodicals.[2] J.E. van der Pek, a young architect who later made his name as a designer of important social housing complexes, was quoted at length:

> "For those who know the work of Mr. W. it came as no surprise that the Stedelijk Museum should represent a new expression of his lack of ability. (...) In truth, it was apparent long before the scaffolding came down that Amsterdam had gained a new piece of failed architecture."

(It's clear that rapid judgments about new buildings are not a new phenomenon in Amsterdam.) Van der Pek concluded that Weissman's sensitivity was "too little developed, so that his works can never be works of art. In order to illustrate this lack of developed sensitivity I will discuss a few fragments of his work, subsequently providing evidence for: a lack of feeling for composition, for contours, for line, for color, for detail, for a sense of truth."

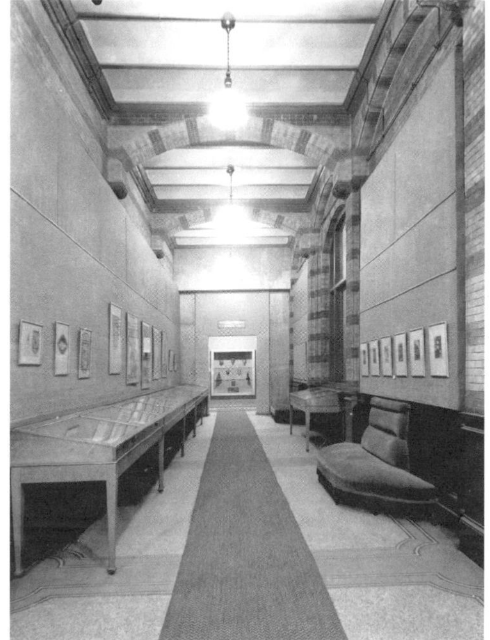

This hall with its display cases for applied arts exhibits provides an impression of the former interior.

1 W. Kromhout Cz, 'Het nieuwe museum aan de Van Baerlestraat te Amsterdam' [The new museum on the Van Baerlestraat in Amsterdam], *Architectura,* 20, number 3 (21 September 1895), 38, p. 67.

2 Een résumé [A résumé], *Architectura* Volume 20, number 3 (19 October 1895), p 181–184.

The same article in *Architectura* quoted a piece from the journal *De Opmerker*, in which an anonymous writer defended Weissman by means of ad hominem criticism of Van der Pek's plea for sensitivity in architecture as naivety:

> "For Mr. Van der Pek it will be the same as for many others: once he attempts to put his ideals into practice he will see them fading away, one by one; if he continues to promote 'sensitivity' as at present he will quickly abandon architecture, wholly disillusioned, and turn instead to writing poetry..."

The appreciation of Weissman by the anonymous author was limited, however. He only went so far in his praise as to say that, "the architect of the Stedelijk Museum in Amsterdam has subordinated his 'sensitivity' to his good sense, and while Mr. Van der Pek may now denounce this, we are persuaded that, had the architect acted otherwise,the resulting building would have been far less suitable than it now is."

This author had a point about the suitability of the building as a museum, and this became clearer still when many of Weissman's interior decorations disappeared into the background when everything was painted over in white. The museum building, so impoverished in the eyes of Kromhout with its lack of articulated artistic expression, turned out to be entirely suitable for the exhibition of contemporary art. Without slipping into the background entirely, the architecture does not compete at all with the art on display. The whitewashing of the interior, associated with Sandberg's name, was one element of a transformation that began in 1937 with a commission to F. A. Eschauzier to alter and expand the existing museum and continued for many years.[3]

Eschauzier was not the first to design an extension to the Stedelijk Museum; his archives contain an unsigned drawing dated October 1915 showing a hook-shaped single storey extension consisting of seven rooms, lit from above and connected to the Garden Hall, which is now known as the Audi Gallery.[4]

The changes proposed by Eschauzier were realized under the close oversight of Sandberg, who was appointed curator under D.C. Roëll.

3 For information on Eschauzier's work see: Jouke van der Werf, *F.A. Eschauzier: Een orde voor de zintuigen* [An order for the senses], Rotterdam 1999, pp. 98–103. The successive structural and spatial interventions under Sandberg's Directorship are summarized in: Frouckje van der Wal, *Experimenten in tentoonstellingsinrichting in het Stedelijk Museum te Amsterdam ten tijde van Willem Sandberg* [Experiments in the layout of exhibitions at the Stedelijk Museum in Amsterdam in the era of Willem Sandberg], Dissertation in Art History, Master's Degree in Modern and Contemporary Arts, Utrecht University, August 2010, Chapter 3.

4 F. A. Eschauzier's archive is held by the Netherlands Architecture Institute in Rotterdam. The inventory code for documents relating to the Stedelijk Museum is ESCH 84-87.

The majority of the proposed alterations were never completed; if they had been made, we would have a very different museum than Sandberg's famous "white Stedelijk". Eschauzier conjured up a fascinating world of graceful forms, subtle colors and delicate details for his client—even the partitions between the urinals were visually extraordinary. Around 1941, Eschauzier drew up various plans in the same style for extensive expansions of the museum on the side facing the Museumplein, but nothing ever came of those, either.

One part of Eschauzier's plan was carried out, however: screens of cheesecloth were installed below the roof-lights on the first floor, the paneling was removed from the exhibition spaces, and the walls there were covered in jute and painted, along with the brick walls of the entrance hall and the staircase. The passageways between the exhibition rooms were also widened. Another important change involved modifications to the form of the galleries on the Paulus Potterstraat. Eschauzier transformed these into tapering spaces using slanting side walls and a sloped ceiling, to maximize the light falling on the (now reduced) rear wall.

The sunscreens are still there, although the system has been changed and they hang higher than before. The galleries still have the form Eschauzier introduced, but the layout of the auditorium on the ground floor, the rebuilding of the Garden Hall to create a reading room and restaurant have not been maintained with the recent renovation and alteration of the historic building. Eschauzier's new wing erected on the Van Baerlestraat in 1954 has also had to make way for the new extension. The same applies to the sculpture garden laid out at the same time, to a design by the municipality's Public Works Department.

Eschauzier designed his own new wing, later dubbed the Sandberg Wing, in collaboration with J. Leupen (head of the Buildings Section of the Public Works Department) and his colleague J. Sargentini. The completed plan was somewhat simpler and smaller than the extensions previously designed for the museum by Eschauzier, and exhibits less of his individual style. The exterior, in particular, owes a debt to Leupen; it appears that Eschauzier concerned himself primarily with the interior.

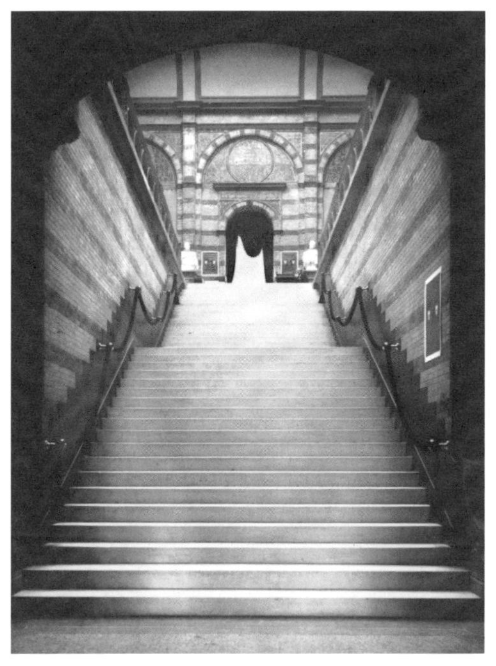

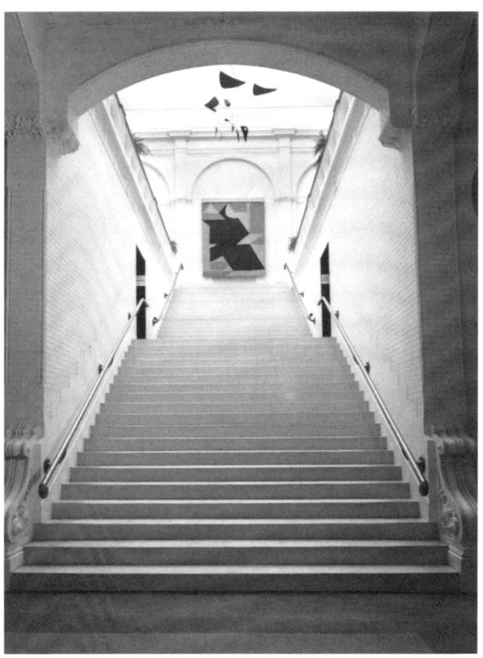

The brick walls of the entrance and the staircase were painted white in 1938.

The use of daylight in the new wing was innovative. The light streamed through both floors on either side through almost fully-glazed side walls, and was controlled by means of blinds. Supplementary light to the lower floor was provided indirectly by lamps pointed at the ceiling. Moveable partitions allowed a flexible demarcation of the space: they were generally placed at right angles to the open façades to provide optimal illumination of the artworks on display.

The extensions to the museum were discussed in the journal *Forum* by Th. H. Lunsingh Scheurleer, an insider. As curator of Applied Arts at the Rijksmuseum he had had dealings with Eschauzier (during Roëll's time as director there, he appointed Eschauzier as architect for renovation work on the Rijksmuseum). The Stedelijk Museum was also familiar territory for Scheurleer: he had collaborated on an exhibition held here in 1941, entitled *In Holland There Stands a House*.[5]

A year after its opening, Scheurleer described the new wing as "an entirely novel solution," breaking with the overhead lighting convention so popular in the nineteenth century in the way that it "prevented troublesome 'shine' on paintings and avoided the worst effects of shadows." Along with these positive attributes of overhead lighting, Scheurleer also said that this source of light "exhibits certain monotonous and unnatural qualities." In the new wing "the light comes in from both side walls, while the artworks themselves take their place either on or together with moveable partitions. This approach has led to an entirely novel use of space, one which we do not hesitate to describe as surprising."[6] Sandberg had an explicit preference for side lighting, as in his opinion most paintings had originally been created under these lighting conditions. A further factor was that the outside world was not closed off in such a transparent exhibition space.

The response to the new wing contrasted in many ways with the reception accorded to Weissman's building, (which, although heavily criticized at its opening, was increasingly valued as time went on). The new wing was greeted with far more enthusiasm and provided a source of inspiration for other museum directors as they planned building projects, But over time it proved to be a difficult space to manage,

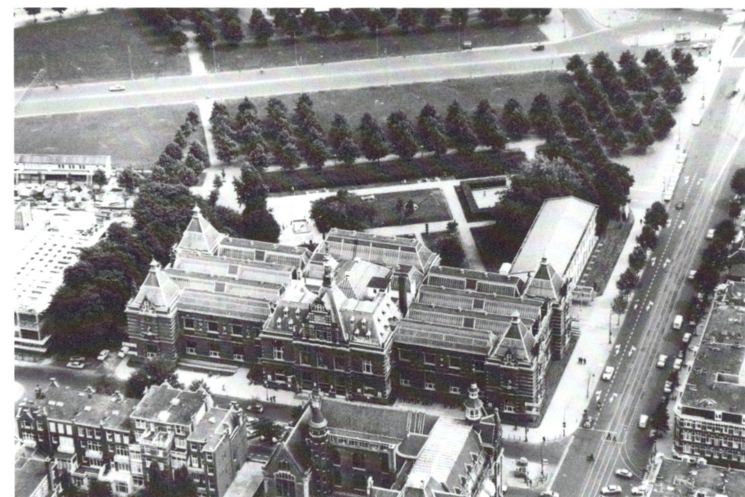

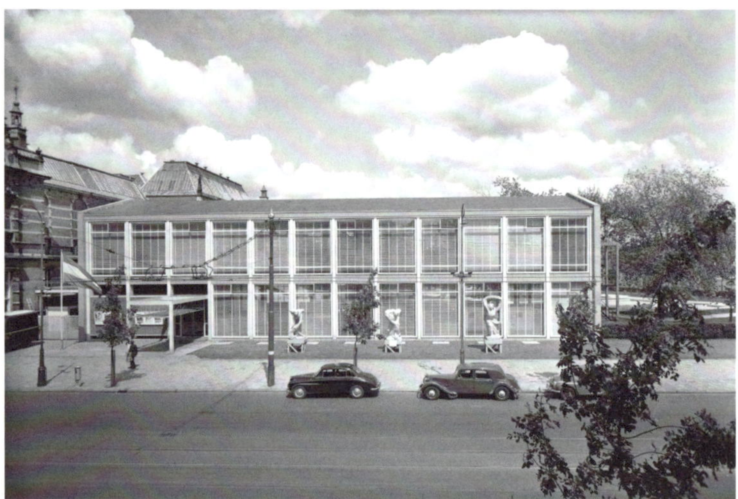

Above: the situation in 1971. Below: the new wing, later also known as the Sandberg Wing.

5 Theodoor Herman Lunsingh Scheurleer (July 22, 1911, 's Gravenhage – August 22, 2002, Warnsveld), Jaarboek van de Maatschappij der Nederlandse Letterkunde te Leiden [Annals of the Society of Dutch Letters in Leiden], 2003–2004. Maatschappij der Nederlandse Letterkunde, Leiden 2005, p. 132–152: p. 135 and p. 138.

6 Th. H. Lunsingh Scheurleer, Het nieuwe tentoonstellingsgebouw van het Stedelijk Museum Amsterdam [The new exhibition building at the Stedelijk Museum, Amsterdam], *Forum* 1955 (11), pp. 370–375, p. 371

with complicating factors such as the abundant incoming light and the limited availability of fixed walls.

Simply put, the new wing was a monument to the most important director in the history of the Stedelijk Museum and to his pronounced museological views. But arguments in favor of preserving that historical vision were no counterweight to the interest in updating that vision with Benthem Crouwel's design, unfortuntely leaving no room for Sandberg's wing. The start of the demolition was marked by an unfortunate incident in which Amsterdam Alderwoman Carolien Gehrels (the city's minister of Art and Culture), rather over-enthusiastically threw a stone through the window of the already-damaged wing as a signal for the renovation project to begin. It was difficult not to see this as an insult to Sandberg's memory.

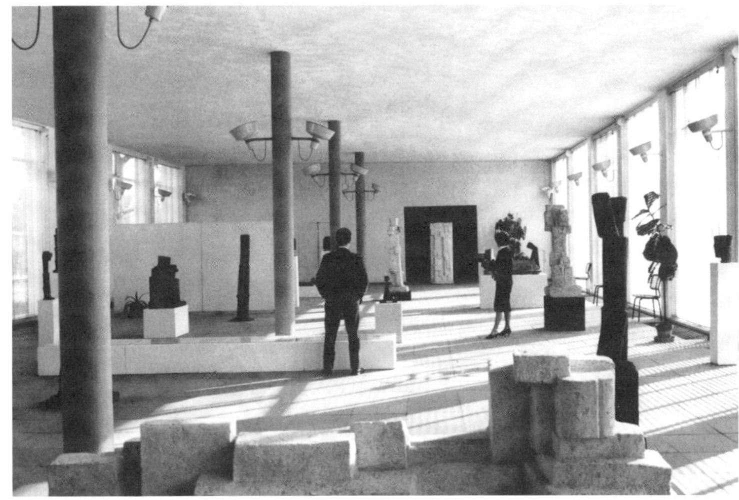
Sandberg had an explicit preference for side light, as in his opinion most paintings had originally been created in these conditions.

With the new wing, Eschauzier's involvement with the Stedelijk Museum came to an end, and from 1955 his work was taken up by his former collaborator Bart van Kasteel.[7] Van Kasteel was responsible for the creation in 1956 of the mezzanine floor, housing the print gallery, (accessed from the staircase landing) where he made ingenious use of the lofty spaces on either side of the stairs. In 1957, he undertook alterations to the Garden Hall, which had been modified by Eschauzier three years earlier. Karel Appel created a mural for this space, his second site-specific work for the museum, following his mural for the coffee bar (1951) next to Eschauzier's auditorium. Van Kasteel was also responsible for the division of the Garden Hall to create a library. The library ran through to the restaurant, with bookcases lining the gallery. He also created office space adjacent to the restaurant, which could be accessed through the bright blue door below Appel's mural. This was followed by a volume containing offices, squeezed in between the library and the new wing, which he connected to the restaurant by means of a transparent passageway. The restaurant was expanded by bricking up the terrace. This is only a selection from the numerous projects initiated by Van Kasteel, who was occupied with building work on the museum right through to the end of the 1970s. One important motivation for his design activities was the ongoing search for (additional) space within the museum for

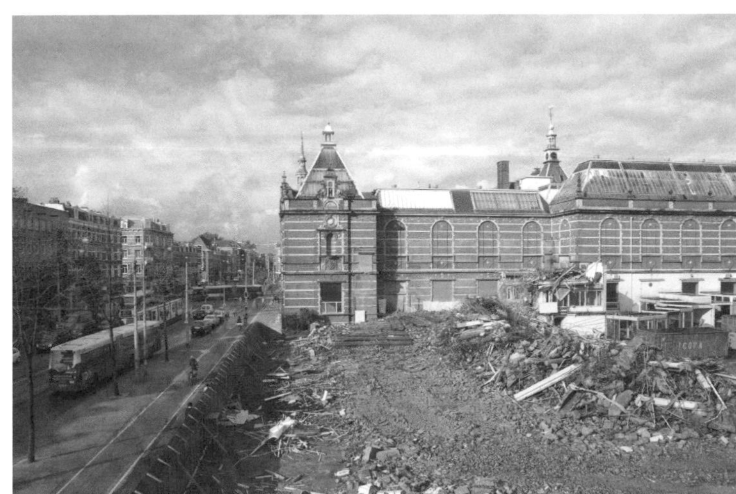
Demolition of the Sandberg Wing in 2006.

7 The archive of Bart van Kasteel, which is still in preparation, is held by the Netherlands Architecture Institute and contains much material concerning his work at the Stedelijk Museum between the mid-1950s and the end of the 1970s.

storage, offices and studios, making use of attics, garrets and mezzanine floors. This was the reason behind his construction of an office building in the gap between the old building and the new wing—an element in what, to his mind, ought to have been a substantial reorganization of the museum building. He also added a new entrance on the Van Baerlestraat, east of the new wing. Only some of Van Kasteel's ingenious ideas for improvements in and around the building were implemented, and now little remains even of what was built. The exceptions include the glazed façades of the former main entrance on the Paulus Potterstraat, which replaced Weissman's massive timber doors around 1960.

The next phase in the history of the building began under Wim Beeren, who was director of the Stedelijk Museum from 1985 to 1993. The desire at that time for a substantial expansion of the museum found favor with the city, which was prepared to release funds for the purpose. In 1992, four architects—Rem Koolhaas, Wim Quist, Robert Venturi and Carel Weeber—competed for the job. Of the four, the only one without a museum design to his name was Weeber. The Kunsthal in Rotterdam by Koolhaas and his Office for Metropolitan Architecture was under construction at that time. Koolhaas was already working on his proposed designs for the competition to build the Netherlands Architecture Institute, as was Wim Quist, who had various museum other buildings and extensions under his belt, including the expansion of the Kröller-Müller Museum. Shortly before 1992, Robert Venturi's practice Venturi Scott Brown of Philadelphia had completed an extension to the National Gallery in London.

The Venturi Scott Brown design was selected out of the four submissions, but two years later the situation changed, when Rudi Fuchs was appointed as the Stedelijk's director. The contract awarded to Venturi Scott Brown was withdrawn and Portuguese architect Álvaro Siza was asked to submit a design for an extension to the Stedelijk Museum. Siza had worked in the Netherlands during the early 1990s, contributing to urban renewal projects in The Hague, and at the time he was working on a residential and office project in Maastricht. He was also responsible for the 1993 Galego Museum of Modern Art in Santiago de

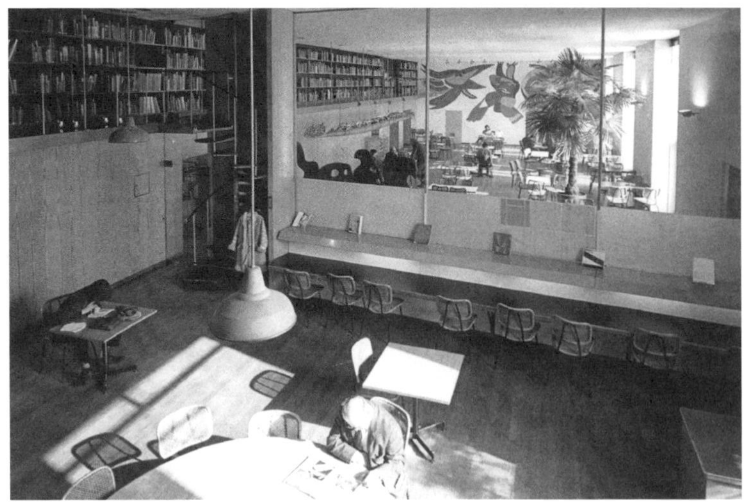

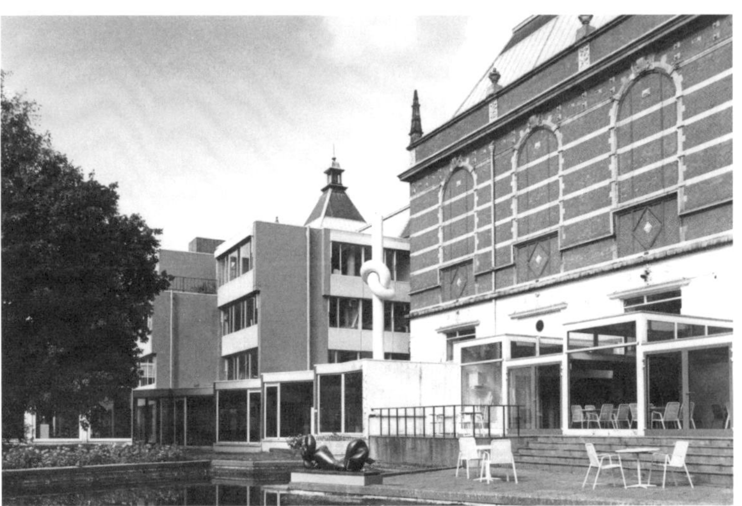

Up until 2004 the library was situated immediately adjacent to the restaurant. This was an initiative by Van Kasteel, who partitioned off a section of the Garden Hall for the purpose. The library ran through to the restaurant, with bookcases lining the gallery.

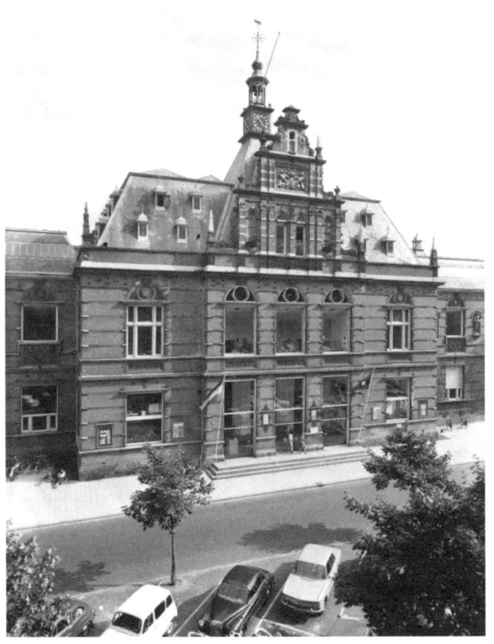

The former main entrance on the Paulus Potterstraat in 1984.

Compostela, and worked on the new building of the Serralves Museum in Porto; its design bore an obvious similarity with his plans for the Stedelijk Museum.

Fuchs' commission of Siza turned out to conflict with new European legislation covering tendering procedures for public works. In a second attempt, the official procedure was followed, with an open call for architects in the European Union to submit proposals; Siza was still appointed, while complying with the rules.

The museum and Siza had to deal with tensions between their ambitions and the available budget. The submitted designs were too expensive, and there were also concerns that his proposed expansion was too "enclosed"—something which perhaps shouldn't have come as a surprise, given Siza's other museum designs. The city resolutely rejected a proposal that Audi should sponsor some of the construction costs, saying it didn't want a "car showroom" in the museum (a nice example of political framing). In the meantime, Siza and the museum were faced with the problem of a grassy rise containing the entrances to the parking lot and the underground supermarket, known as the "dog's ear", which Danish landscape architect Sven-Ingvar Andersson had devised as an element of his layout for the Museumplein. This feature did have some significance in relation to the square, but for the Stedelijk it was an inconvenient obstacle.

In 2003, the City of Amsterdam decided to withdraw the contract awarded to Siza and start over. A committee chaired by Martijn Sanders, an art collector and then-director of the Concertgebouw, devised a new schedule of requirements, which was to form the basis for a new call to tender in the summer of 2004. Five Dutch architectural firms were asked to submit sketch designs, in accordance with the European rules for the tendering process. They were Herman Hertzberger, Claus en Kaan Architecten, Henket & Partners, Diederen Dirrix van Wylick Architecten and Benthem Crouwel Architects.

The brief covered both renovation and expansion of the museum. The jury was chaired by Herman van Vliet of the municipality's Physical Planning Department. Van Vliet had served as

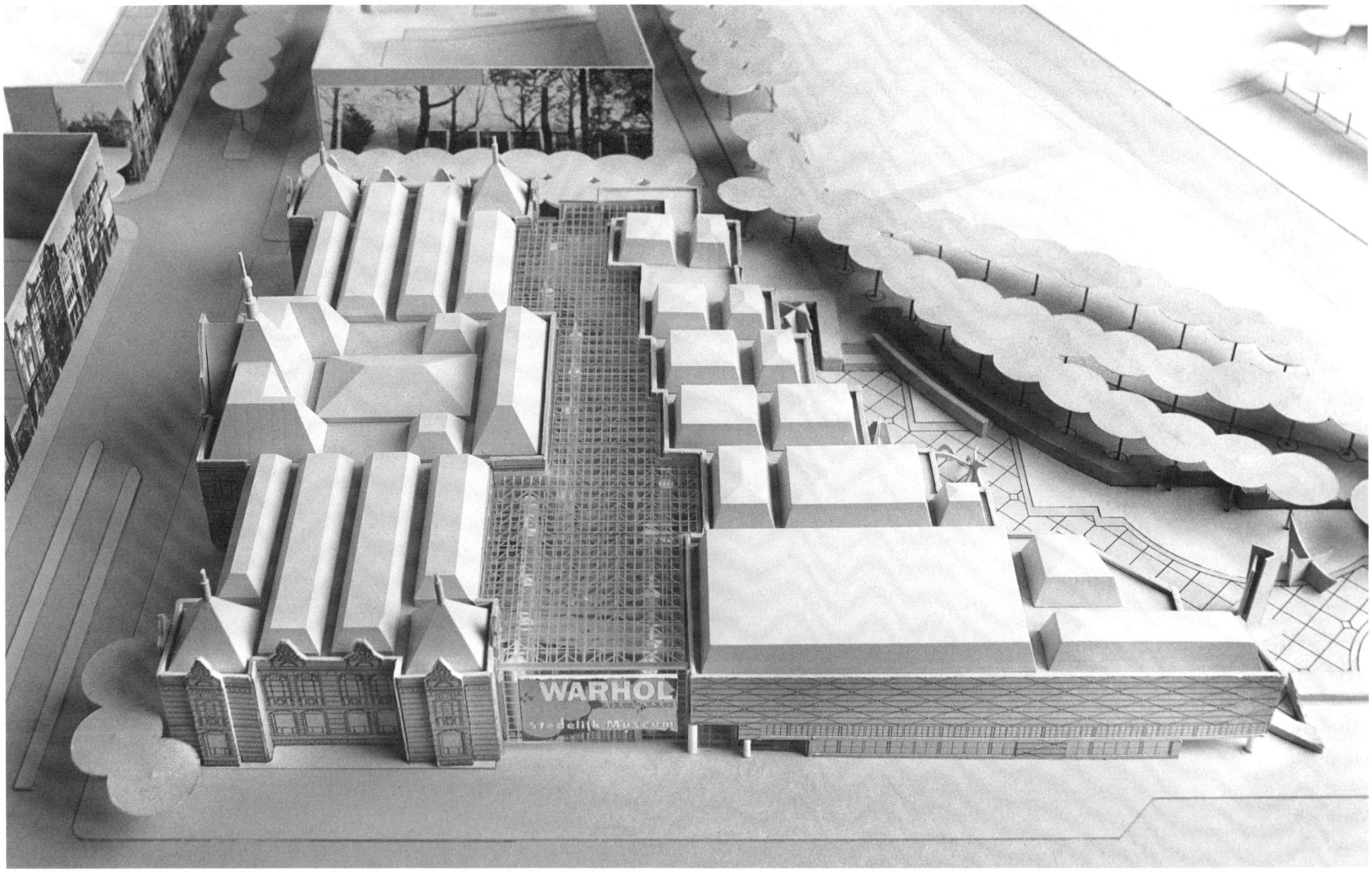

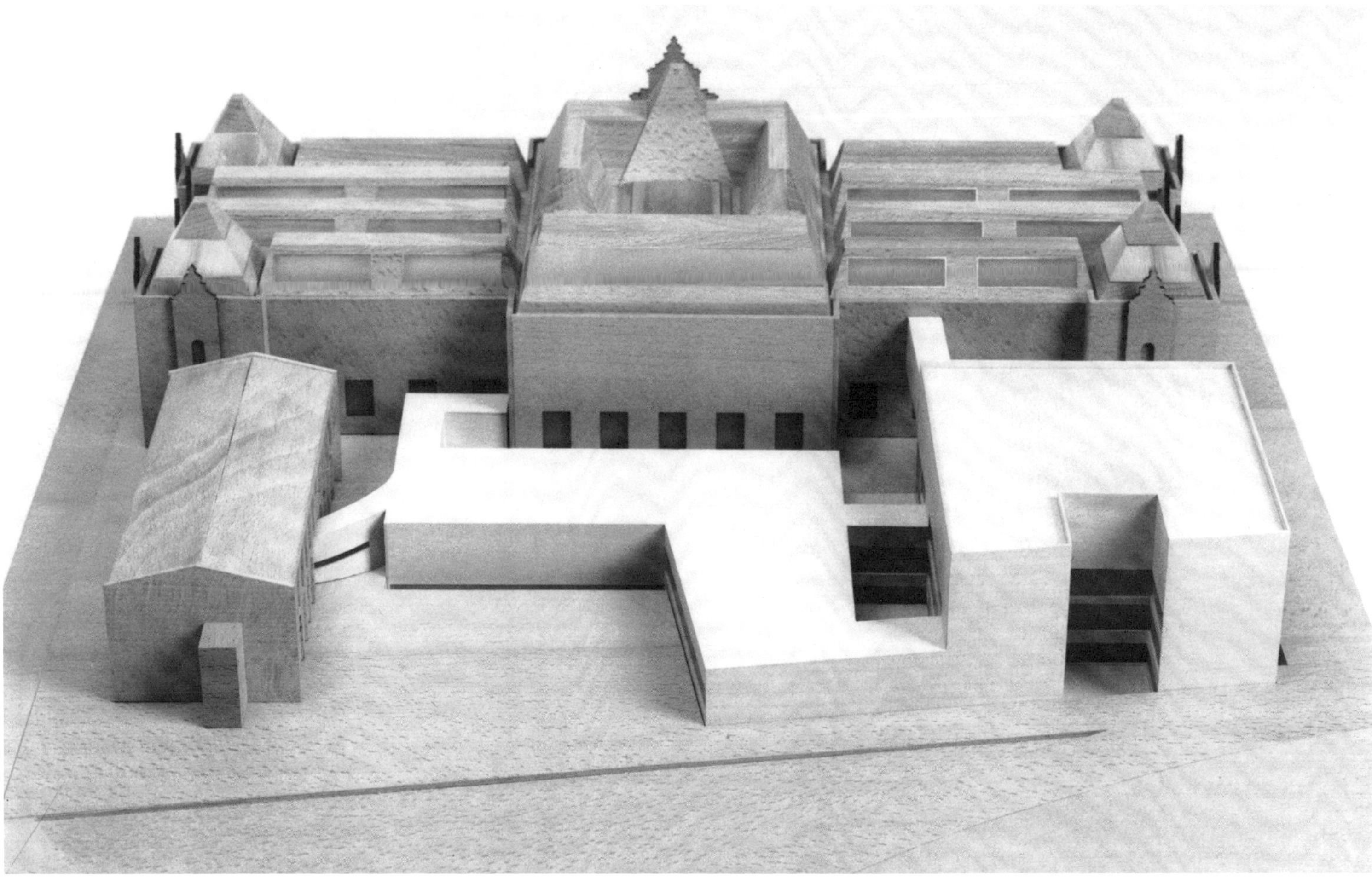

Venturi Scott Brown drew up a design for an extension to the Stedelijk Museum in 1992 (above), but the situation changed with the appointment of Rudi Fuchs as director and Álvaro Siza was then asked to submit his design (1997).

the project leader during the transformation of the Museumplein between 1996 and 1999. The other jury members were Maarten Kloos (director of the ARCAM architecture centre), journalist Max van Rooy, Wim Pijbes (then-director of the Kunsthal Rotterdam, and since 2008, director of the Rijksmuseum), artist Toon Verhoef, the then-acting director of the Stedelijk Museum, Hans van Beers, and two architects, Wim Quist, who had competed for the contract in 1992, and Sjoerd Soeters.

The jury was unanimously persuaded by the plans submitted by Benthem Crouwel Architects:

> "Benthem Crouwel have succeeded superbly in giving form to the concept 'unity in duality'. This is a question of architecture. Benthem Crouwel have further succeeded in turning the face of the Stedelijk Museum towards the Museumplein. This is a question of urban planning. With their design, Benthem Crouwel have proved themselves masters of both these disciplines. The implementation of the Benthem Crouwel design will be something to rejoice in."[8]

The Amsterdam City Executive and the Stedelijk Museum's supervisory board agreed with the jury's assessment and awarded the contract to Benthem Crouwel. The museum had closed the doors to the Paulus Potterstraat in anticipation of the renovation and expansion project, and also because the permit for use had expired in 2003 and had not been extended.

In May 2004, the museum found a temporary refuge in the as-yet un-demolished part of the post office on the Oosterdokseiland, named Post CS. The building was made suitable for exhibitions with minimal modifications by Zwarts & Jansma Architecten, and the museum remained there until the demolition began in the late summer of 2008. Repeated delays to the renovation and new-build work meant that the Stedelijk Museum had to manage for four years without a museum building. The museum staff was housed in a former cigarette factory in Amsterdam-Sloterdijk during this time.

During the expansion and renovation of the building, there was also the question of storage. The collection was spread across two

8 Juryrapport architectenselectie Stedelijk Museum [Jury report on the selection of architects for the Stedelijk Museum, 31 August 2004]. www.stedelijkindestad.nl/pages/ontwerp

depots in Amsterdam and one outside the city. Claus en Kaan had already developed a design for a building to house the collections in Amsterdam-Noord. This did not go forward, but in its place came a new Stedelijk storage facility in the western harbor area, created in 2009 based on a design by Dedato, a bureau with a reputation for creativity and efficiency in the construction of commercial premises.

In the eight years that elapsed between the award of contract to Benthem Crouwel in the summer of 2004, and the official opening in the summer of 2012, the museum was faced with a series of setbacks. The public did not respond positively to the design of the new building, although the criticisms fit with the longstanding Amsterdam tradition. And there were many complaints about the long absence of the Stedelijk Museum; these were understandable, although the museum countered this with the observation that with the Post CS building and activities around the city, the museum had hardly been absent. There were also construction delays, cost overruns, budgetary problems, and a lot of political wrangling. The contractor went bankrupt, and the building

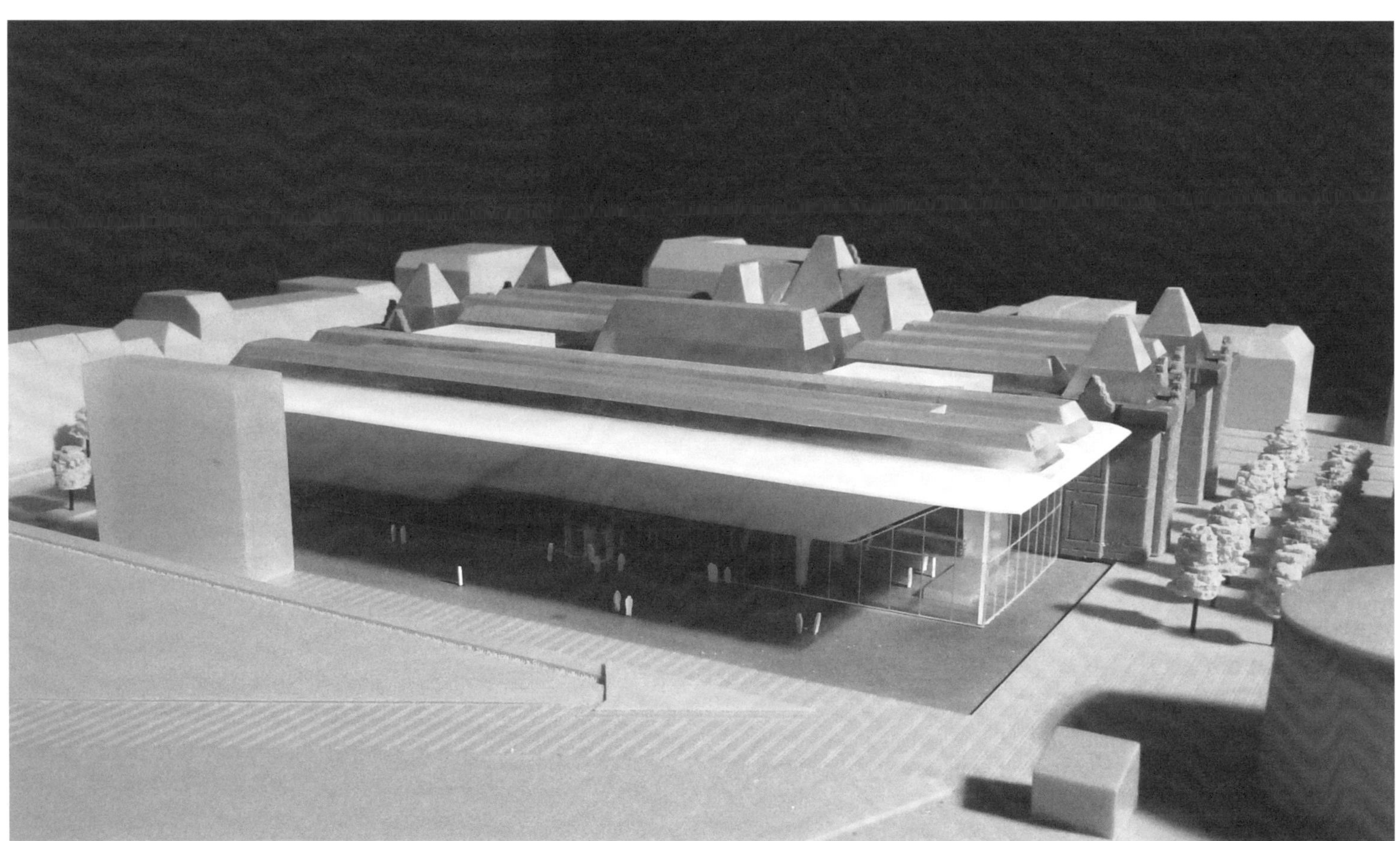

A maquette of the design by Benthem Crouwel Architects. "Benthem Crouwel have succeeded superbly in giving form to the concept 'unity in duality'."

suffered 400 thousand euros worth of damage when disorderly football fans climbed on it while celebrating Ajax's championship win in 2011.

Despite all this, the renovated and expanded Stedelijk Museum opened to the public once again on 23 September 2012. Weissman's structure has been restored to its place as the essence of the museum as a building for exhibitions. All the rooms that had become clogged with other functions have been stripped down, all the later additions have been demolished. The interior has been further simplified and made lighter, in line with Sandberg's philosophy. Virtually all of the changes made from the Sandberg era up to the temporary closure in 2003 have been reversed, with only a few exceptions: the addition of Appel's murals, Eschauzier's gallery designs and Van Kasteel's glazed façade on the former entrance on the Paulus Potterstraat. This erasure of the intervening renovations has left a building constructed in two phases: 1895 and 2012. This is the essence of the "unity in duality" so praised by the jury, although the notion might perhaps be disputed on historical grounds. The approach taken is very similar to the work of Cruz y Ortiz at the Rijksmuseum, where intervening phases (to designs by Wim Quist and the same Eschauzier who was so significant to the Stedelijk Museum) have also been stripped away.

The "duality" aspect of the new Stedelijk Museum is particularly evident on the outside. The updated museum consists of two separate buildings, differing in form, color, composition, materials, transparency, tectonic expression and detail. The distinction between them is emphasized by the optical separation of the new and old buildings and the minimal physical contact between them. The aspect of "unity" is expressed primarily in the interior, with exhibition spaces in the extension completed in the same manner as the renovated rooms in the older building.

The building has, in a sense, been turned around by Benthem Crouwel. The entrance has been relocated from the Paulus Potterstraat to the Museumplein, which was also the back garden of the Van Gogh Museum and the Rijksmuseum. This "reversal" of the Stedelijk

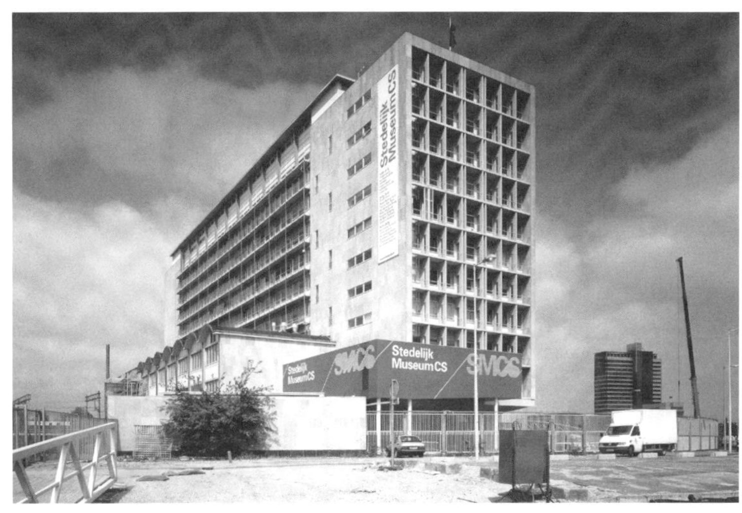

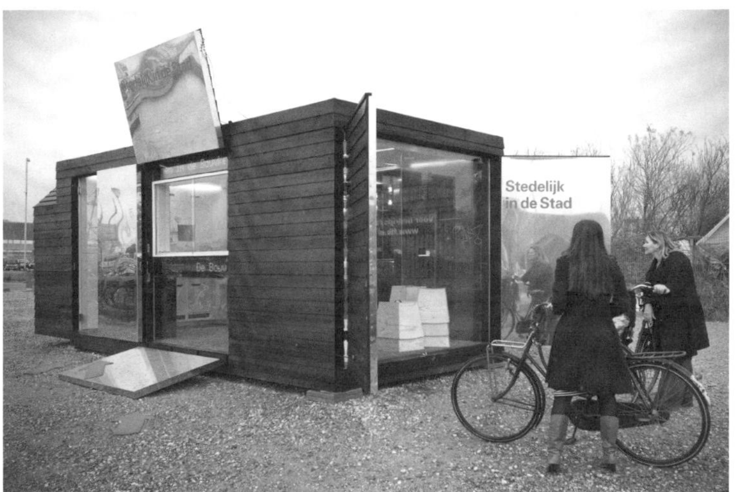

Above: the Post CS building on the Oosterdokseiland. Below: the "Construction Cabin", a mobile space used for museum activities around the city.

Museum prompted the Van Gogh Museum to consider creating its own entrance on the Museumplein side, which can be expected to further change the use and significance of this square.

The power of the architecture of the new Stedelijk Museum lies in its clarity, a trademark of Benthem Crouwel Architects. This applies both to the manner in which the older building has been reduced to its essence, an enfilade of exhibition rooms surrounding a central staircase, and also to the manner in which old and new stand side by side as two individual elements. And it also applies to the ingenuity with which the programmatic diversity of the new building has been united and ordered, with a central role given to the visitor's perspective.

The distinction between old and new relates not only to the appearance but also to the fundamental order of the structures. Where in Weissman's building the classical rules of symmetry provide a harmonious balance, the new building is characterized by an order more closely resembling what you might find under the hood of a car: a complex configuration intended to achieve optimal performance in the most efficient manner possible. The quality of a car is not determined solely by its internal and external appearance; cars can only properly be evaluated by their usefulness. And so it is with the architecture of the Stedelijk Museum, which unmistakably possesses a comfortable and practical elegance, but which truly comes into its own in its capacity as a museum that attracts the public.

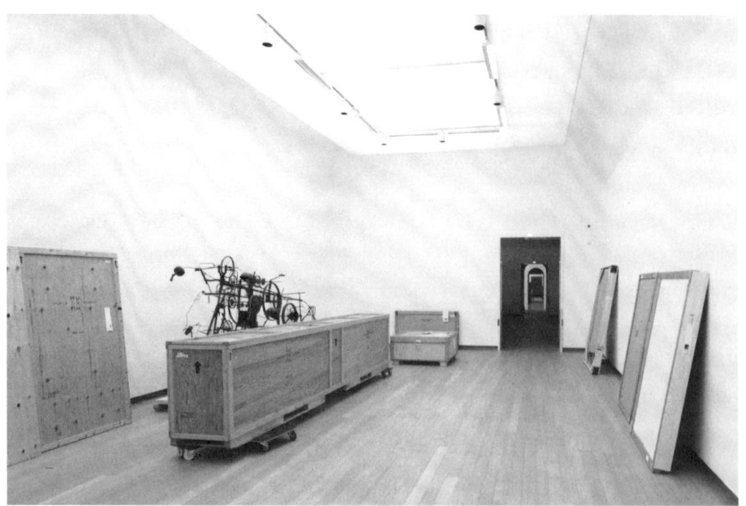

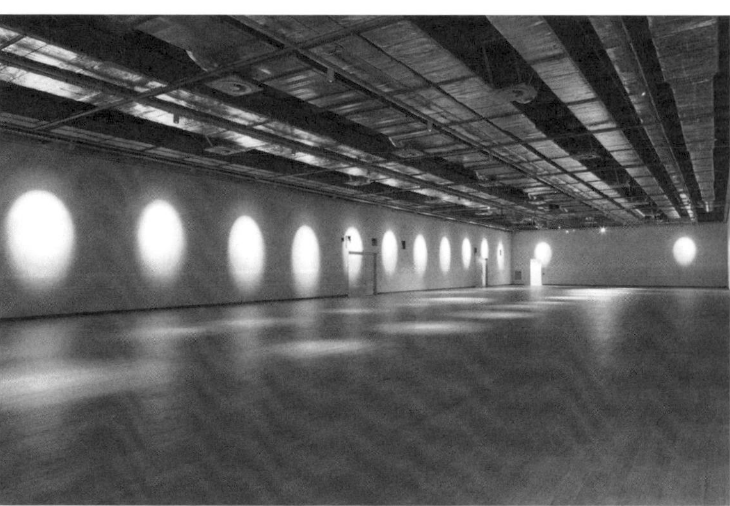

Above: the renovated interior of the old building. Below: the large exhibition space on the lower floor of the new-building, the ABN AMRO Gallery.

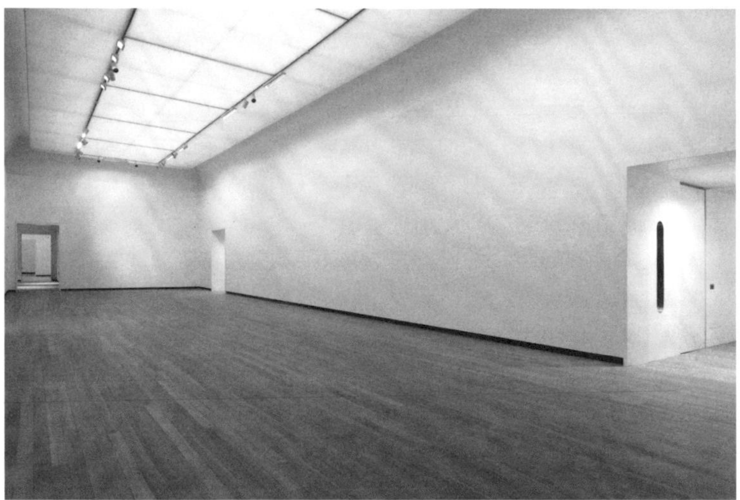

The VandenEnde Foundation Gallery, counterpart to the old building's Hall of Honor. "The distinction between them is emphasised by the optical separation of the new and old buildings and the minimal physical contact between them."

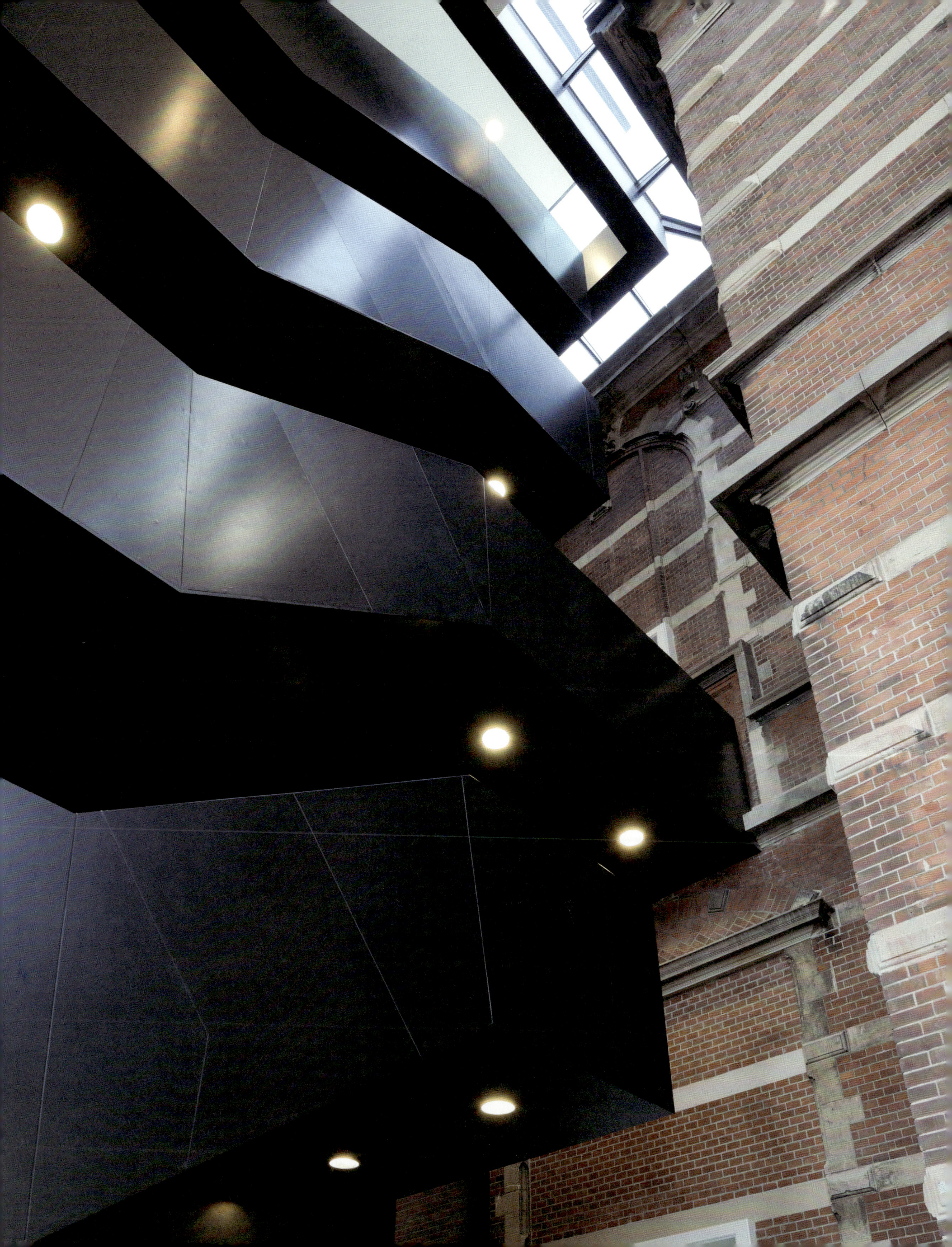

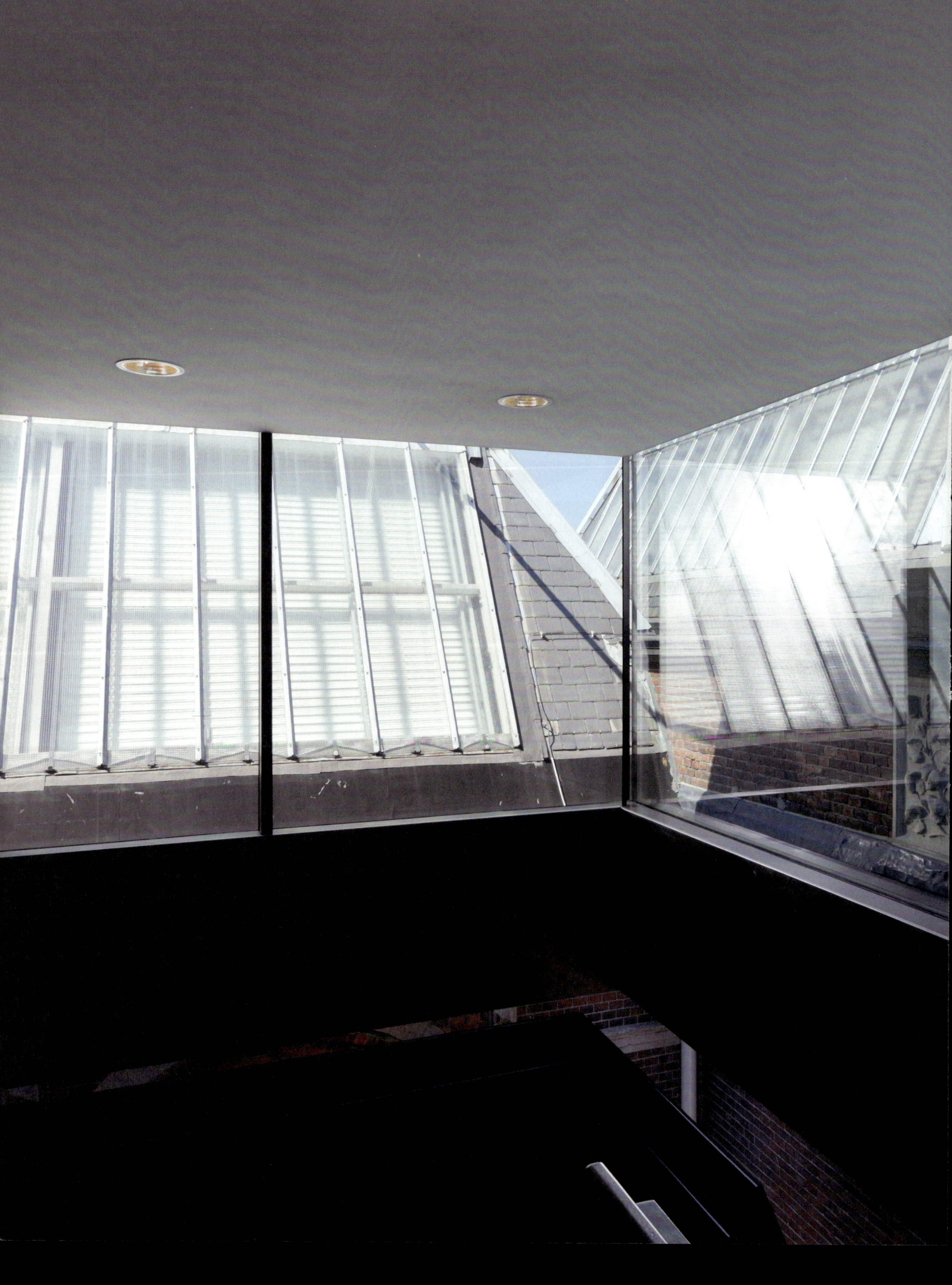

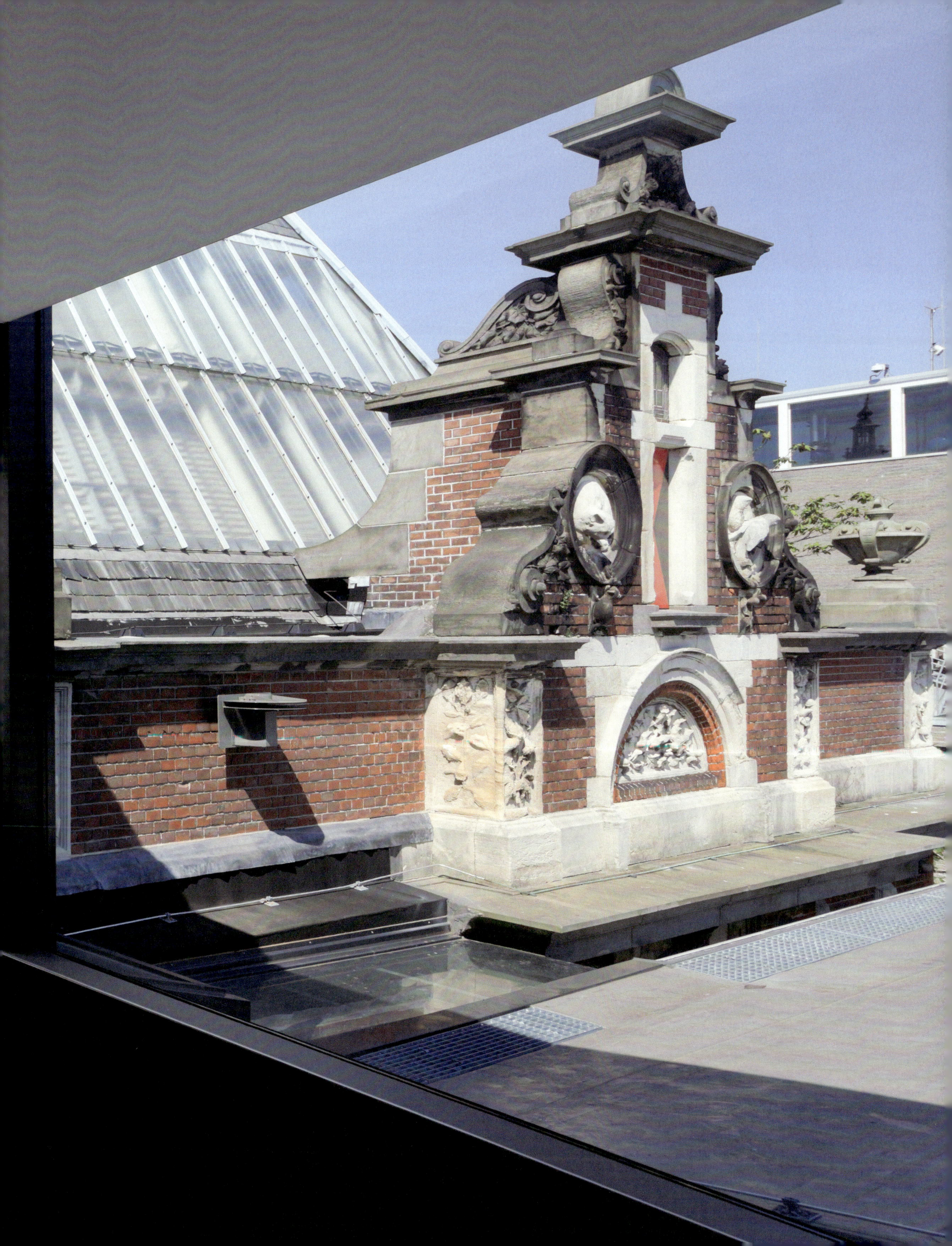

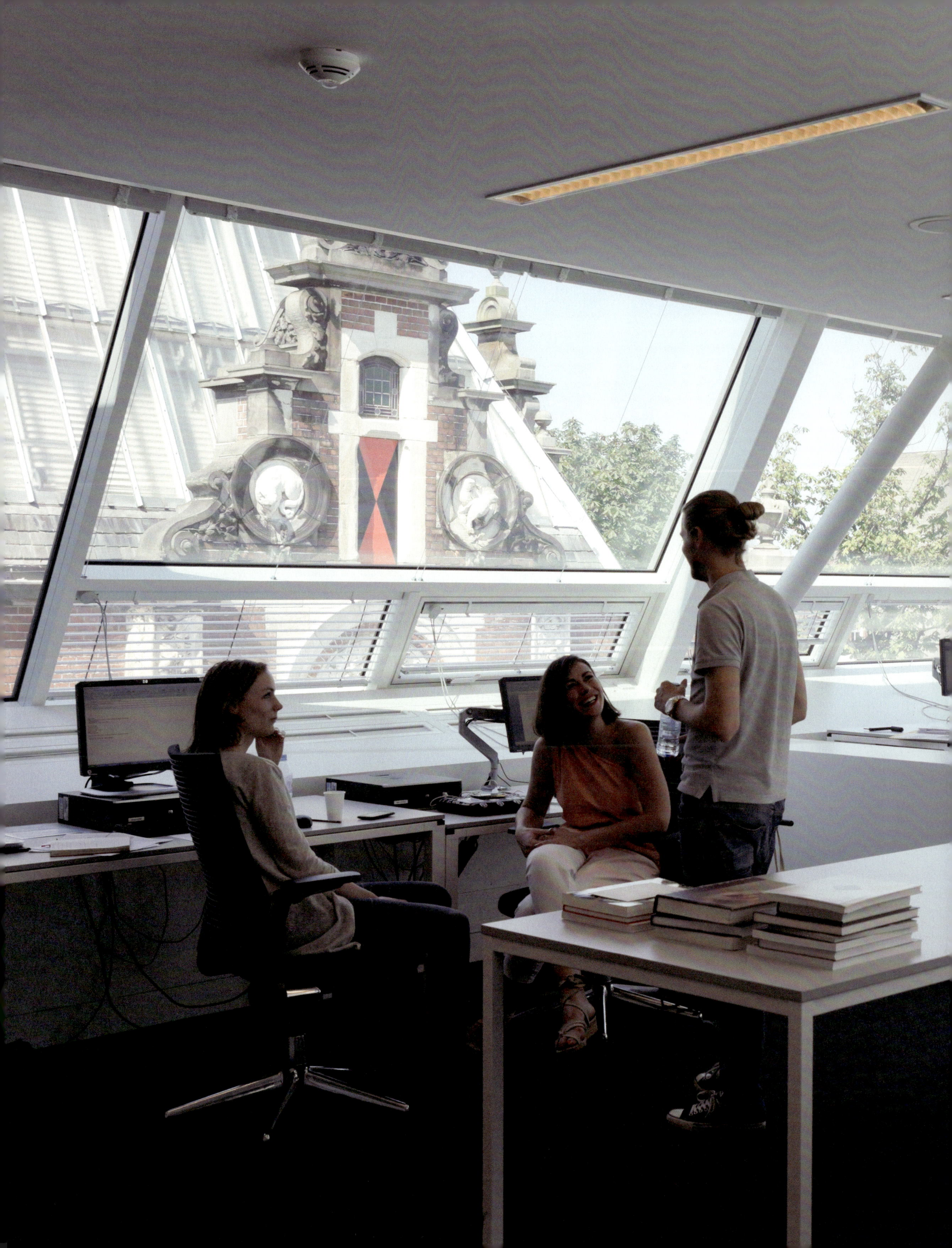

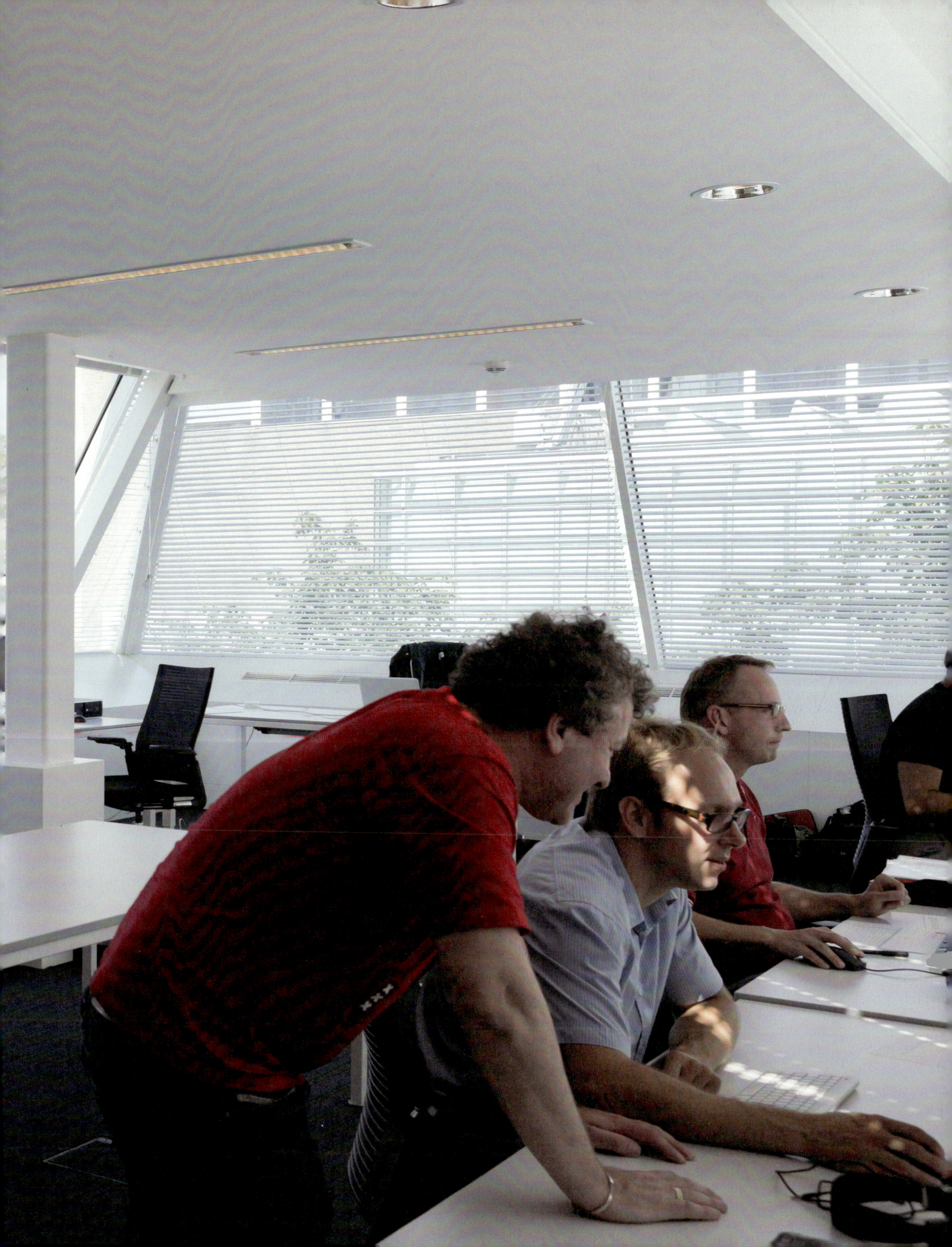

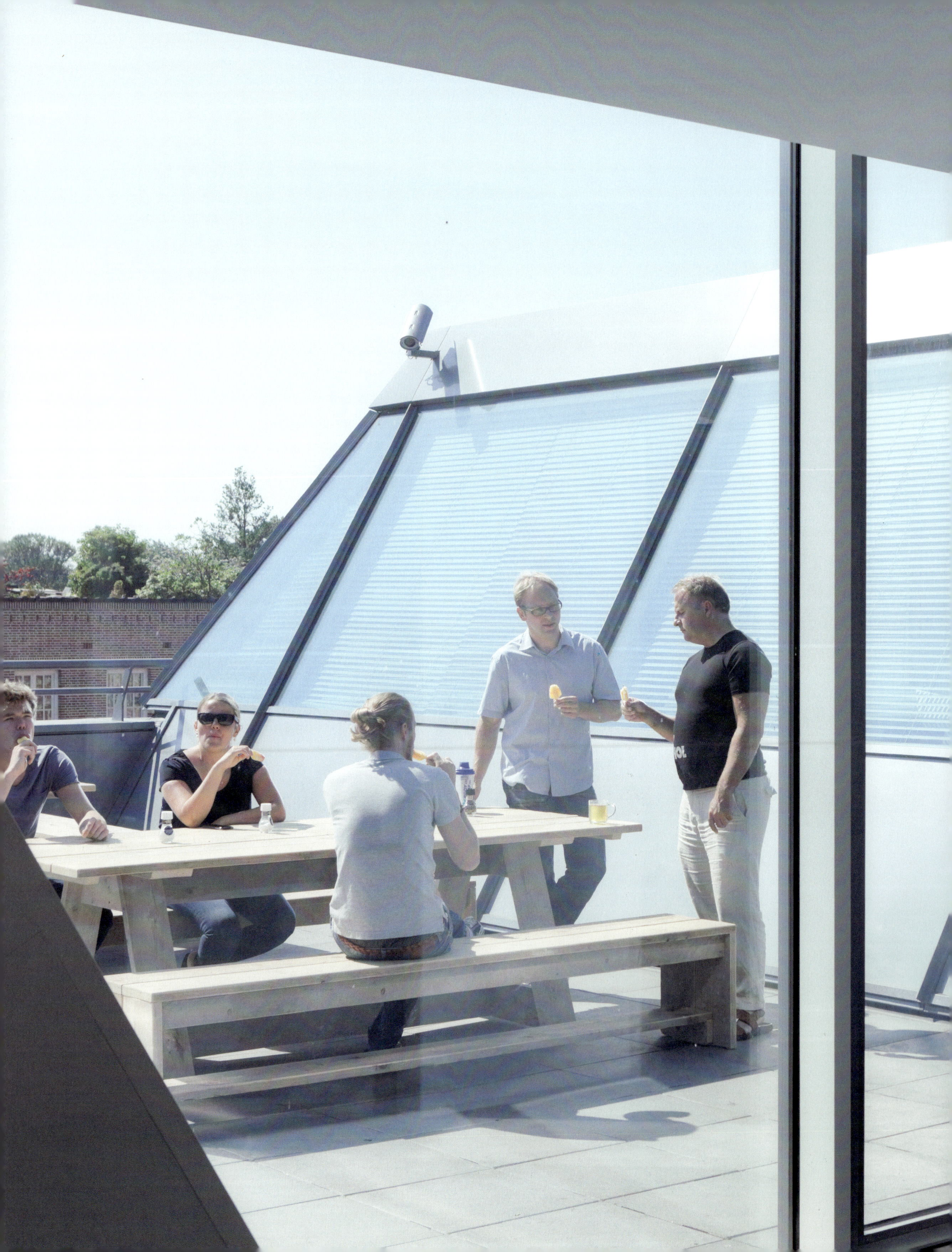

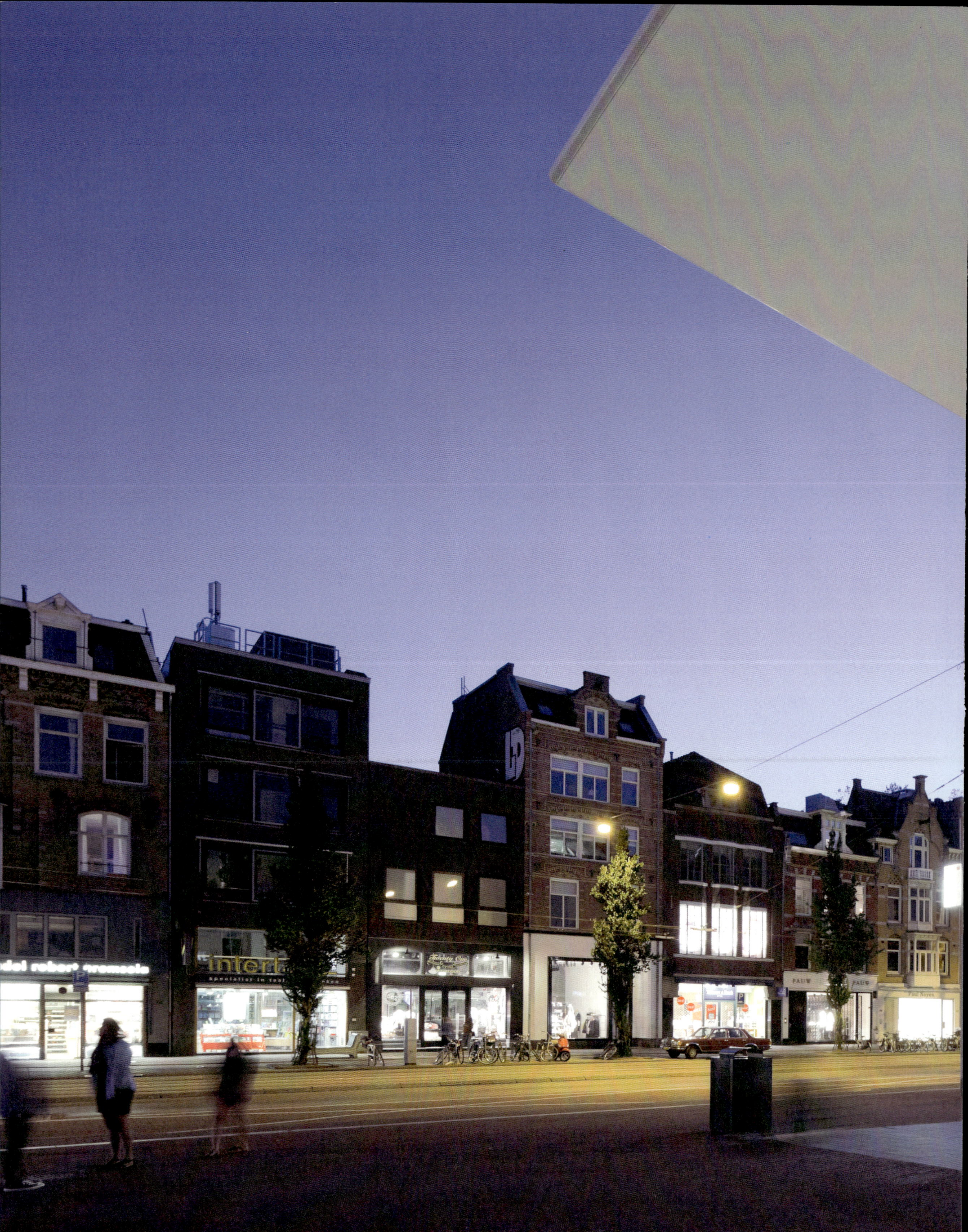
PAUW

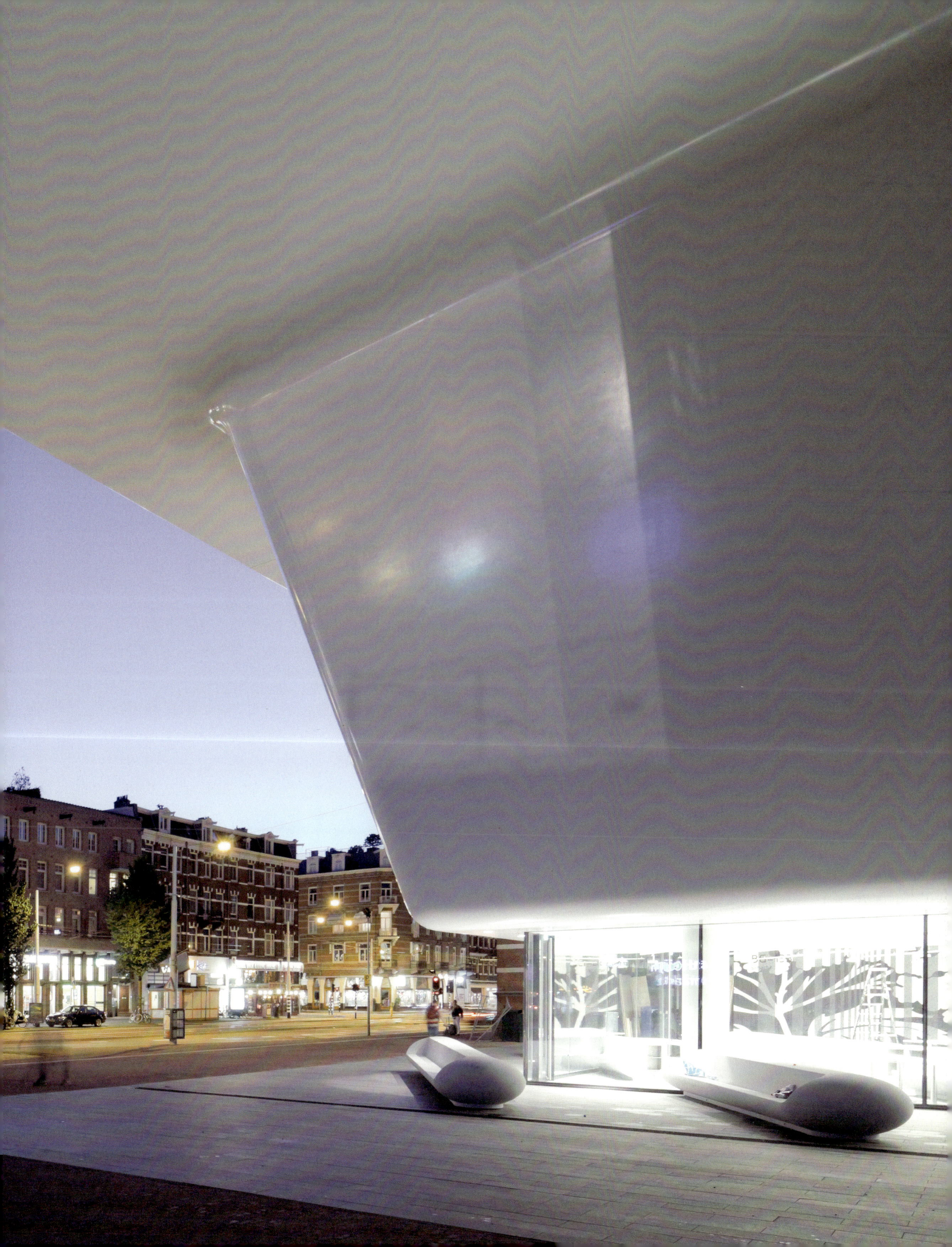

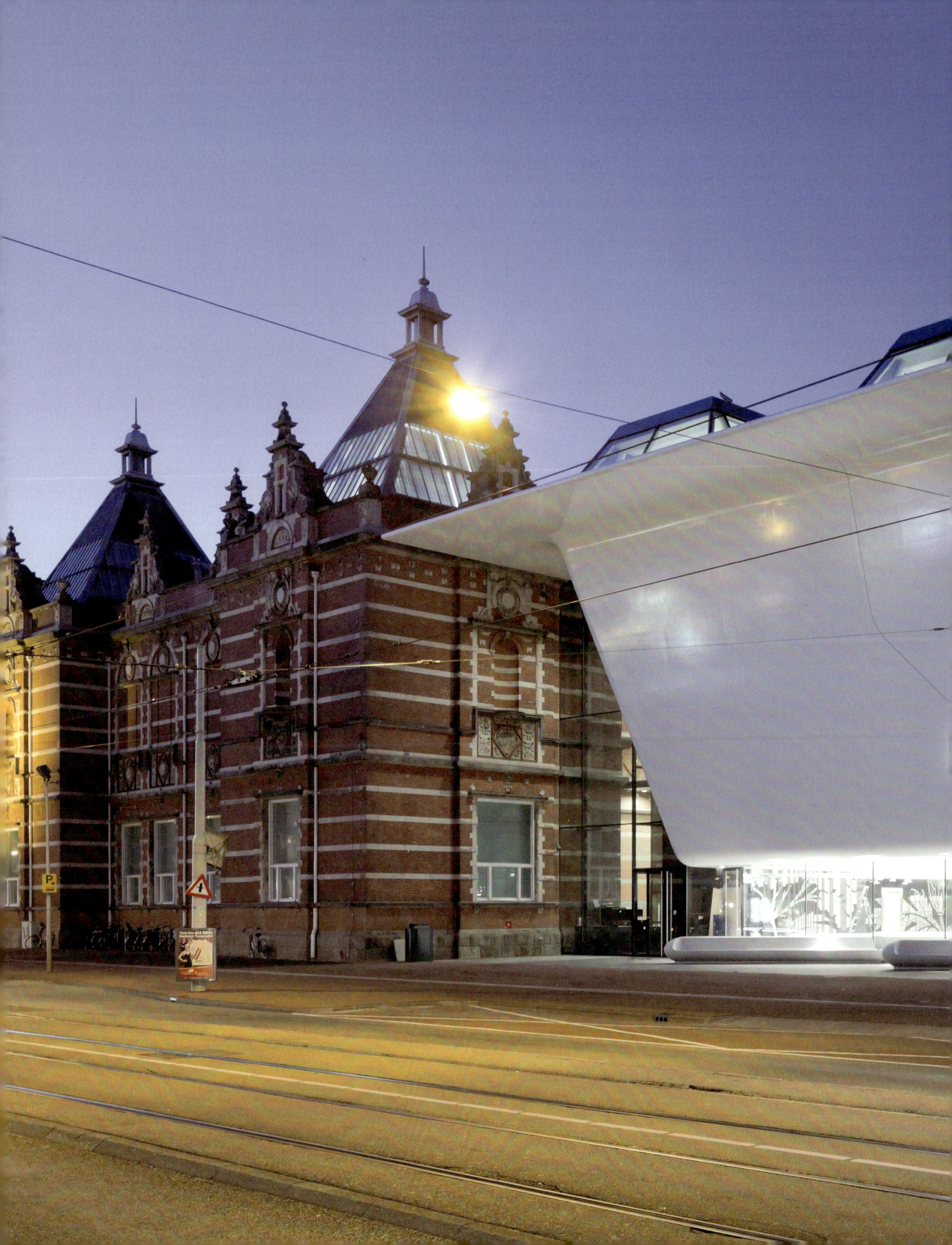

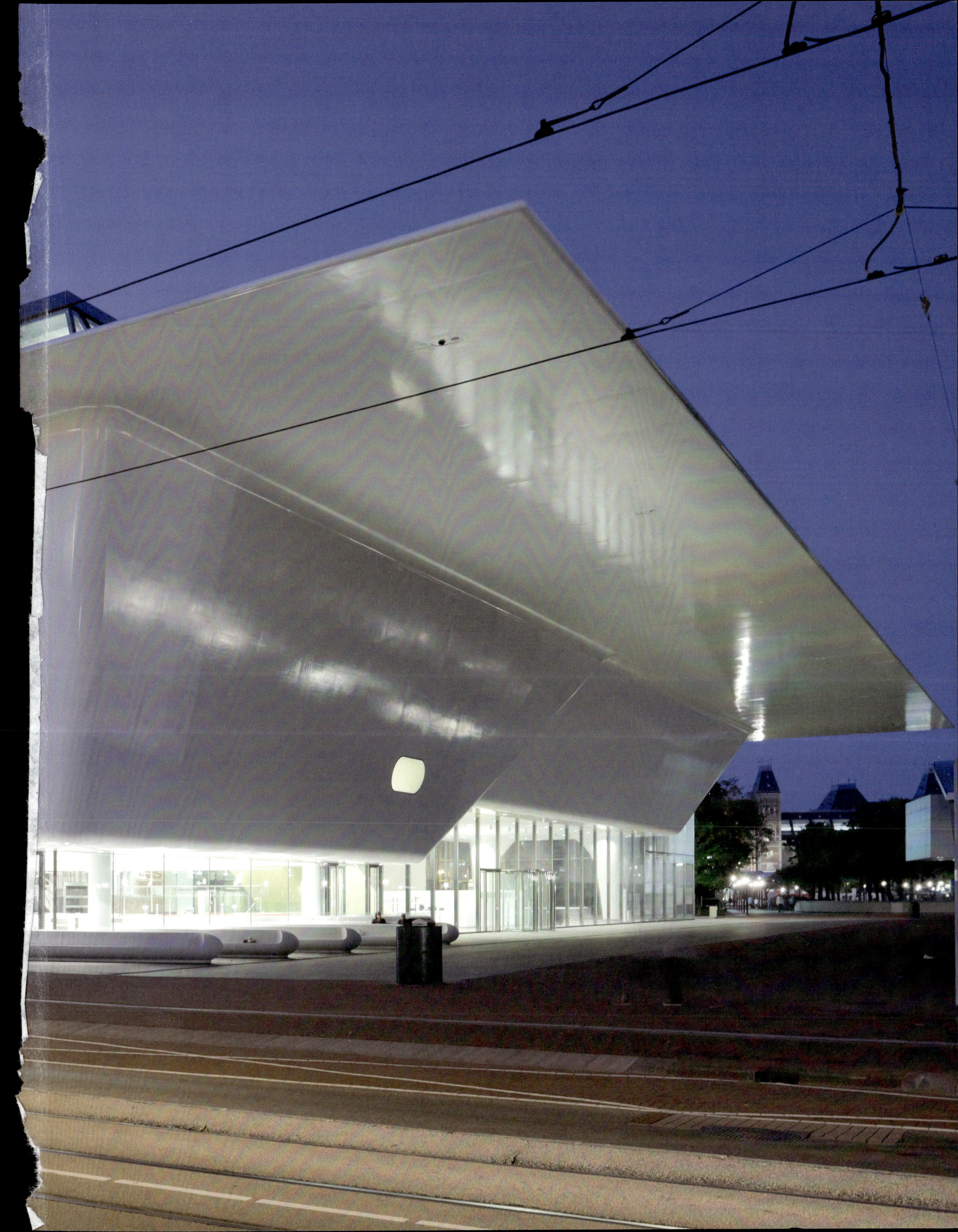

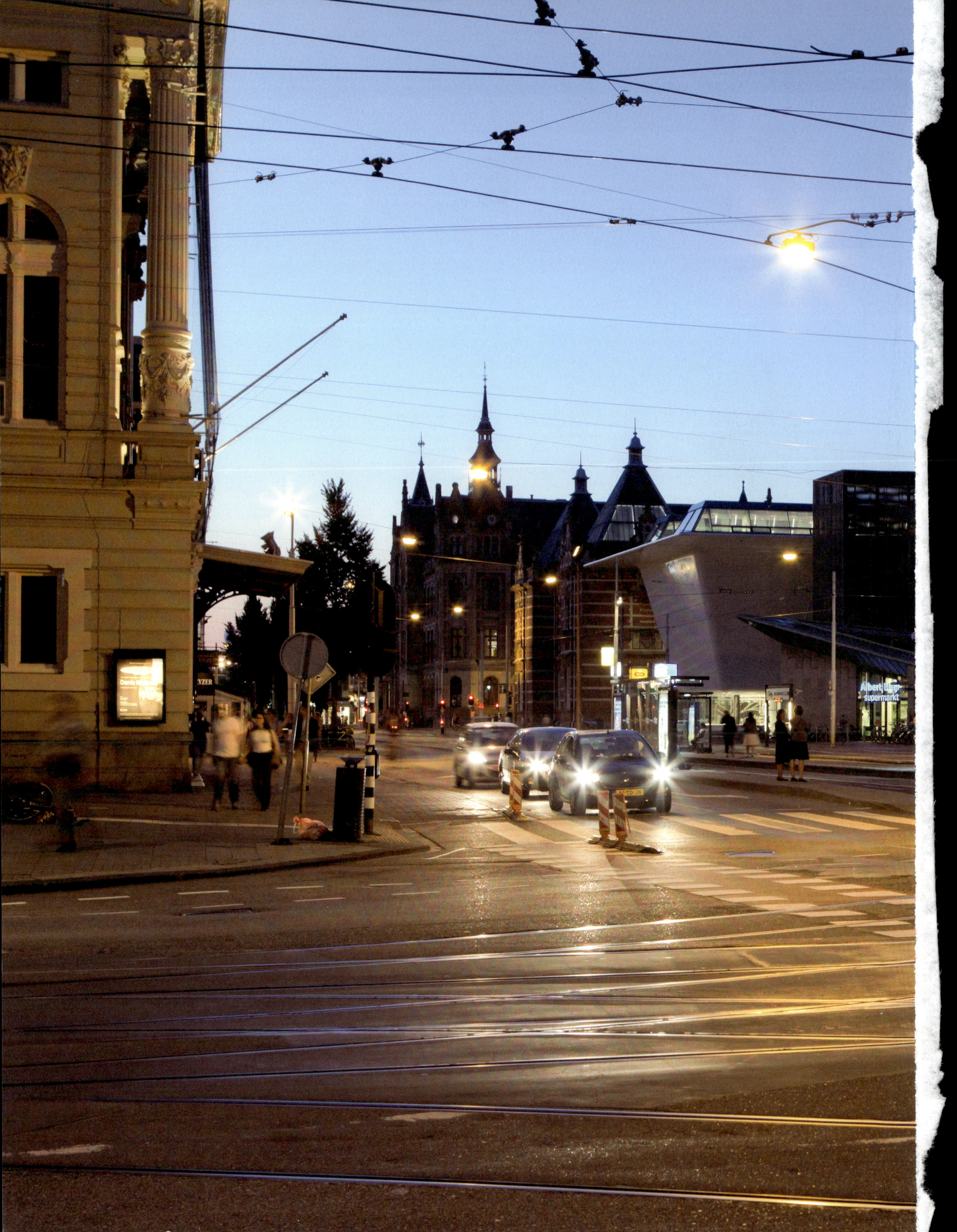
Albert
supermarkt